Chris Stacey
and
Darcy Sullivan

First published in 1988 by Boxtree Limited

Text copyright © Chris Stacey and Darcy Sullivan 1988

ISBN 1 85283 206 1

Acknowledgments

Photographs appear by permission of:

Alpha: 58(tr), 60, 65, 79, 82, 117(br), 117(bl), opp.128; (Alan Davidson) 23, 24(t), 59, 90, 95, 98, 103, 106, 116(br), 117(bl); (Steve Finn) 109; (Holtz/ Michelson 69, 81; (David Parker) 25, 56, 72, 104, 105.
Channel 4/Brookside: 89, 92, 93
Grundy: 113, 114
Larkfield Printing: 42
Syndication: 15, 18, 19(t), 19(b), 20, 21, 24(bl), 26, 27, 28, 30(t), 30(bl), 32, 33, 34 & 35, 37, 49, 53, 54, 57, 58(bl), 62, 63, 64, 67, 73, 75(tl), 76, 78(br), 77, 78, 97, 101, 102, 107, 108, 116(tr), 117(tl), 118(tr), 118(br), 119(tl), 119(br), 121(tl), 121(br), 122, 123(tl), 123(tr), 124, 125, 128, 129, 130, 131, 132.
TV Times, Transworld: opp. 32, opp. 33, 36, 38(t), 39, 84, 85, opp. 112, opp. 113, 119(tr).
Yorkshire, Transworld: 45, 46 (tl), 46(b), 47, 48, opp. 48, opp. 49, 117(tr), 127.
Front jacket: TV Times (tl), Syndication (tc), (ml), (mr), (bl), (bc), (br), Alpha (Alan Davidson) (tr).
Back jacket: TV Times.

Designed by Groom and Pickerill
Typeset by York House Typographic
Printed in Italy
for Boxtree Ltd, 36 Tavistock Street, London WC2E 7PB

Published in association with Independent Television Publications Ltd

Contents

Preface

Welcome to Supersoaps, a look at the biggest and best soap operas on British television. While writing it I uncovered many little-known facts about these programmes, which I hope you will enjoy.

I was shocked last year to hear that *Crossroads* will be cancelled, and offer the chapter on this series as a keepsake for the programme's many disappointed fans. Like many of you, I was also stunned to learn the sad news that Jean Alexander (Hilda Ogden) will no longer continue on *Coronation Street* – she was one of my favourites and no doubt one of yours as well.

For me, writing *Supersoaps* has been like appearing in each of the soaps. It's been like walking down Coronation Street, checking in at Crossroads, lifting a glass at the Queen Vic, riding at Emmerdale Farm, brunching at Southfork, dining on *Dynasty* and in bovver at *Brookside*. I hope you enjoy it as much as I have.

Chris Stacey

1
The Origin of
Soaps

Soap operas – we grow up calling them that, and after a few years it seems a perfectly reasonable name, like 'science fiction' or 'sitcom'. But if you've ever asked yourself where the name comes from, you've probably drawn a blank. Why soap operas?

In fact, the origin of this name takes us back to the beginnings of the genre in 1930s America. The country at that time was radio-addicted (as filmgoers will know from Woody Allen's *Radio Days*), hunched around huge wooden boxes that thrilled listeners with *Inner Sanctum*, *Jack Armstrong, the All-American Boy*, *The Shadow* . . . and such proto-soaps as *Ma Perkins* and *The Romance of Helen Trent*, continuing dramatic series about star-crossed lovers and secret affairs whispered over the tuneful breezes of violins.

These programmes were broadcast, like all such shows in America, on commercial radio glutted with commercials. Soap manufacturers such as Proctor and Gamble sponsored several of the series – perhaps because they were 'cleaner' than rough-and-tumble mystery programmes. Radio producers nicknamed the programmes 'soaps' and the name caught on with the press.

Television began replacing radio as family entertainment in the 1950s, and as the more successful radio soaps jumped from the airwaves to the small screen, 'opera' was added to 'soap' as a joke on the programmes' 'heavy' fare. Soap companies still sponsor the programmes in America, though few

programmes have sole sponsorship. One of the early soaps, sponsored by Sweetheart soap, was *One Man's Family*, which was on NBC from 1949 to 1955.

Not all the old shows are dead, either. The daytime soap *Search for Tomorrow* has been on television since 1951, making it the world's longest running soap. Like many American daytime soaps, it's transmitted five days a week. Back in the 1950s the programmes lasted only fifteen minutes and most of the action took place over the phone as budgets were very small and the programme was transmitted live.

Americans seem to enjoy excess, and presently there are eleven hours of soap operas on the television each day, mostly between 10 a.m. and 3 p.m. There is literally more soap than any one person could watch, especially as they overlap each other across the three major television networks. Together, these shows are watched by some 45 million Americans.

These daytime soaps are more like UK soaps than *Dallas* and *Dynasty* – they're shot on videotape, portray 'realistic' people and rarely stray beyond a fixed number of sets. Because a show like *General Hospital* (whence sprang Emma Samms of *The Colbys*) lasts an hour and there are five new episodes a week, these series must be shot incredibly fast. The harrowing schedules allow little time for retakes, so fumbles, mumbles and awkward pauses keep amused viewers on their toes.

Beginnings in Britain

The BBC has never been much for poaching from American radio, so it wasn't until the 1950s that British soaps hit the air, with series such as *Mrs Dale's Diary* and *The Archers*. Still running today, *The Archers* invaded listeners' homes on New Years Day 1951, and stayed there to become one of the most popular radio programmes of the 1950s and 1960s. Indeed, the BBC used its popularity in the rating war against ITV – when the new television network debuted on 22 September, 1955. *The Archers* kept many families away from the telly with a stable fire that killed the well-liked Grace Archer.

Britain entered the television soaps field a few years after America. Associated Rediffusion's *Sixpenny Corner*, with Howard Pays and Patricia Dainton as garage owners, ran fifteen-minute episodes five days a week in 1955. One of its begetters was Hazel Adair, later a founder of *Crossroads*. And the popular *Emergency Ward 10* appeared twice weekly on ITV from 1957.

In December 1960, Granada TV launched *Coronation Street*, transmitted live in the North as a local programme, set to run for thirteen weeks. The rest is history.

The amazing success of *Coronation Street* prodded Hollywood into developing a soap-style show for 'prime time' (7 p.m. to 11 p.m.). The ABC television network came up with *Peyton Place*, a loose adaptation of Grace Metalious's novels. Shown twice a week in more than thirty countries, this programme starred later film names such as Ryan O'Neal and Mia Farrow, and became so popular during its 500-episode run from 1964 to 1969 that the term 'Peyton Place' is still used to mean a tangled web of romantic relationships. *Peyton Place* was also the first soap to have spinoffs: the series *Return to Peyton Place* (1972–4), the TV movie *Murder in Peyton Place* in 1977, and the reunion *Peyton Place, The Next Generation*, a 1985 TV film.

Coronation Street's success also encouraged other British producers to develop series, including supersoaps *Crossroads* (1964), *Emmerdale Farm* (1972), *Brookside* (1982) and *EastEnders* (1985). These shows have been joined on the airwaves by American contenders *Dallas* (1978), *Dynasty* (1980), *Knots Landing* (1981), *Falcon Crest* (1981) and *The Colbys* (1985).

Not all the soaps, though, are British or American. Besides soapesque series such as *Châteauvallon* from France, the UK has begun screening Australian soaps in the daytime. Series such as *Young Doctors*, *Sons and Daughters* and *Neighbours* often seem as ludicrous as the 1970s American comedy spoof *Soap*, but can be no less compelling than our own series.

As the runaway success of *EastEnders* showed, the soap opera is far from a dead medium. In the early 1980s, cable television allowed American viewers to see a soap/sitcom called *Brothers*, an adult-oriented programme about two brothers, one of whom is gay, and their family. In addition, ITV's coffee-time service introduced Britain to the US soap *Santa Barbara*, and *EastEnders* is now shown in the States.

Soap Appeal

Soap operas are among TV's most successful series, but there still aren't as many of them as there are, say, sitcoms. Why aren't there a rash of inferior soaps vying for the huge ratings? One reason is that it's difficult for a new show to gain a toehold. Series such as *Angels*, *Triangle*, *Weaver's Green* and *Albion Market* have failed to catch on.

That's not surprising, really, when you consider what draws people to soap operas in the first place. Most television series have individual episodes with a beginning, middle and an end. Soap stories never end – if anything, they multiply, from *Dallas* to *Knots Landing*, *Dynasty* to *The Colbys*. A viewer tuning in for the first time is lost in a forest of unknown faces, complicated relationships and incomprehensible innuendos.

But once you sort out the plots, you're hooked – soaps have the never-ending change and complexity of life, and regular viewers are drawn into another world. It's this vicarious aspect that, according to Kenneth Lee, a top NHS psychotherapist and clinical psychologist, makes soaps so fascinating. Whether in the polished glitter palaces of *Dynasty* or the gritty side streets of *EastEnders*, we see lives that we almost believe in, friends we come to care about, and quite possibly, a fictional version of ourselves.

2
Coronation Street –
The King of the Soaps

On-screen, the saga of *Coronation Street* began with Mrs Lappin, owner of the corner shop since 1918, telling new owner and ex-barmaid Florrie Lindley, 'Now the next thing you want to do is get a sign writer in.' Off-screen, Britain's most popular soap opera began with a tall twenty-two-year-old named Tony Warren and a two-year-old television company named Granada.

Building *Coronation Street*

When Warren walked into the casting offices at Granada in 1958, he was looking for boyish roles, the only kind he had played to date. Casting director Margaret Morris disheartened him by saying he was too old and too tall to go on playing misunderstood teens. But she perked up when Warren talked of his writing, because Harry Elton, a Granada colleague, was scouting for writing talent.

Thus, the young Tony found himself turning out episodes of *Shadow Squad*, a detective thriller with Rex Garner. Within six months he was moved to Granada's promotions department, where he made trailers and wrote scripts for the continuity announcers. Unfulfilled by these assignments, Warren sent the BBC a pilot script called *Our Street*, but the BBC never responded. It was the last time Warren's writing would be ignored.

Whilst trying to adapt *Biggles* for TV, Warren told Elton he was fed up and begged to be taken off the project. 'Let me write

about something I know,' Warren said. This struck a responsive chord in Elton – as one of the fledgling independent television companies, Granada's charter was to make programming that reflected their transmitting area, from Liverpool to Scarborough in the north. *Biggles*, though entertaining, somehow missed the mark.

Elton told Warren to write a story set in Salford, and he'd evaluate it. Finally inspired, Warren created a show called *Florizel Street* overnight, peppering it with characters and situations he had observed in northern towns. Elton liked it, and after Warren completed three more episodes Elton told Sidney and Cecil Bernstein, who ran Granada, that he had the makings of a good series.

The Bernstein brothers allowed Elton to carry on and make two pilot episodes, while Warren was instructed to write a thirteen-instalment run for the series, including a conclusion where the street was bulldozed! Elton became executive producer, Stuart Latham became producer, Dennis Parker became the designer and Harry Kershaw was brought in as an additional writer.

They had the crew – now to find the street. Though most of the taping would be done live in the studio, the credits and outdoor establishing shots would set the mood of the area. Warren toured Salford and found the suitable Archie Street. Granada studio 2 was booked for 9 December 1960, 7 p.m.; the pilot would go out live, then after a fifteen

minute break the second episode would be pre-recorded. Based on the success of these two episodes, *Florizel Street* would live or die.

Actually, it almost died before that. Advertisers, concerned about the slightly scandalous nature of a realistic working-class show, threatened to pull their commercials from the time-slot, effectively killing the programme. However, a pilot made exclusively for Granada's bosses satisfied them that the show was worth an initial investment.

One major change, however, would be made before 9 December; quite obviously, the name. Granada executives found it wanting, and asked around to see if other people felt the same. Their suspicions were confirmed when a Granada tea lady said Florizel Street sounded like a disinfectant! By group consensus, the name was changed to *Coronation Street*, a title which gave the show an extra touch of class.

A Legend Begins

'Every door hides a story in this new twice-weekly serial,' ran the entry in the *TV Times*. 'There are seven front doors and more than

Some of the original (1960) cast of Coronation Street. *Back row: (l to r) Ivan Beavis (Harry Hewitt), Jack Howarth (Albert Tatlock), Ernst Walder (Ivan Chevski), Philip Lowrie (Dennis Tanner), Alan Rothwell (David Barlow), Arthur Leslie (Jack Walker), un-named, Frank Pemberton (Frank Barlow), Noel Dyson (Ida Barlow), Margot Bryant (Minnie Caldwell).*
Front row: Doris Speed (Annie Walker), Bettie Alberge (Florrie Lindley), Anne Cunningham (Linda Cheveski), Pat Phoenix (Elsie Tanner), Violet Carson (Ena Sharples), Christine Hargreaves (Christine Hardman), William Roache (Ken Barlow), two un-named, Lynne Carol (Martha Longhurst).

twenty interesting people. Come down *Coronation Street* on Wednesdays and Fridays and join the neighbours.' Those who followed this advice on 9 December were intrigued, though the press reaction varied. The *Guardian* said '*Coronation Street* will run forever,' but the *Daily Mirror* was less impressed: 'The programme is doomed from the outset of its dreary signature tune.'

15

What caught viewers' imagination, and clearly bored the *Mirror* reviewers, was a frank and fresh tone, mixed with local humour and believable drama. Even Granada, which in theory served the north, recruited its actors and actresses at the time from London, and the airwaves were largely devoid of northern or working-class accents. British drama and films, such as *A Kind of Loving*, had already crossed this class line, but for television *Coronation Street* was an important step. Indeed, many of those who tuned in late to that first episode, missing the 'dreary signature tune', thought they were witnessing a documentary about life in the north!

Coronation Street was also an important step for Granada. Soon networked on ITV, it overcame the objections of late subscribers Tyne Tees and ATV Midlands to become Britain's longest running TV serial, sold to seventeen countries around the world and seen by over 250 million viewers. Most foreign countries see the English with foreign subtitles – in Hong Kong these are in Mandarin Chinese, with the characters displayed down the left side of the screen.

The programme has employed more than 100 writers during its 28-year run and some 2,000 actors! Twenty-three characters have died, nine have been born and there have been twenty-four marriages. An estimated 20,820 pints have been drunk in the Rovers Return pub (perhaps one-third of them by Stan Ogden). And the corner shop has made about 9,100 balm cakes – so if any of the actors put on weight, you know why.

Stories from the Street

The excitement begins in the series' first month, when Ena Sharples, the mission caretaker, is caught drinking in the Rovers and a fractured gas main threatens the Street's inhabitants. Elsie's daughter Linda gives birth to a boy. Ken Barlow gets a 2nd class honours degree in English and History. Harry Hewitt marries Rovers' Irish barmaid Concepta Riley. Ena fights the council, which wants to rename the street Florida Street, and writes to Prince Philip. Elsie has an on-off affair with sailor Bill Gregory. Linda and her husband leave for Canada. In 1963 Jerry Booth marries Myra, and Dennis

Tanner gives Annie Walker an embarrassing 'This Is Your Life'. In 1964 Hilda and Stan purchase No. 13 for £575. Elsie is held up at gunpoint; and Ken and Val Barlow produce twins.

Elsie begins a two-decade on-off affair with Len Fairclough. Harry and Concepta return to Ireland, while Lucille stays on and lives at the Rovers. No. 7, the Hewitts' old home, collapses; Lucille is thought to be inside but is later found. Elsie meets and marries American GI Steve Tanner; Harry Hewitt returns for the wedding and is killed repairing his car. Maggie and Les Clegg buy the corner shop; their son Gordon has an affair with Lucille. Les, an alcoholic, goes into a mental home. Len is accused of murdering Steve Tanner but is later cleared. Val Barlow is held hostage in her new tower block flat. Alan Howard appears in the Street.

The next few years bring several disasters to *Coronation Street*. In 1967 a train crashes over the side of the viaduct. This almost costs Ena her life but she is saved by David Barlow, Ken's brother. Two years later a coach nearly kills several Street residents. In 1971 Val Barlow is electrocuted and dies.

In the early 1970s Elsie's lovers include Len Fairclough, bookie Dave Smith and Alan Howard. Ken marries Janet and Stan Ogden is fined £200 for drunken driving in a Rolls Royce. Betty Turpin joins the Rovers. David Barlow and his son Darren are killed in a car crash in Australia. Irma is brought home to the Ogdens. Billy Walker opens a garage. Alan and Elsie marry but he goes bankrupt and is offered a job by Billy. The ladies of the Street win a trip to Spain and Billy dates Deirdre Hunt.

Emily marries Ernest Bishop. Len buys a sweetshop and installs Rita as manageress with Mavis Riley as her assistant. Elsie goes to London to visit her son Dennis in prison. She is knocked down by a taxi in Oxford Street and temporarily loses her memory. Alan traces her and brings her home. Ken marries snobbish Janet. Maggie marries Ron Cooke and leaves the Street. Fire destroys the mail order warehouse. Bet, barmaid of the Rovers, has a nervous breakdown. Edna Gee dies and Fred goes to work as pot man at the Rovers. After living with Alan in

Previous page *Annie and Jack Walker of* Coronation Street *who ran the Rovers Return.*
Above *The most famous pub in the world, with Elsie Tanner, its sex symbol.*
Below *The cast of* Coronation Street, *with Hilda's 'pinny'.*

Newcastle, Elsie returns alone to the Street.

In 1975 Deirdre marries Ray Langton and two years later their daughter Tracey is born. Rita marries Len Fairclough. Ken Barlow suffers further tragedy when Janet takes a fatal drug overdose, and Emily joins him in grief the next year when her husband Ernest is shot dead. Several characters escape death when a lorry crashes into the front of the Rovers Return.

Towards the end of the 1970s Bet is kidnapped for Rag Week – the ransom is £20 but the Rovers only collects £4.56! Gail and Brian Tilsley marry and soon have a child, Nicky. Alf Robert's wife Renee, owner of the corner shop, is killed in a car crash. Emily gets remarried – to Arnold, a bigamist.

Bet and Elsie chase the same man. Ken and Deirdre marry in 1981, the third time round for unlucky Ken. Two years later Deirdre fixes her eyes on Mike Baldwin but eventually remains with Ken. Bet and Jack Duckworth have an affair; his son Terry later gets Andrea Clayton pregnant. Even Mavis is raving it up, with two men pursuing her, almost marrying one of them, Derek.

Fred marries Eunice, hoping Newton & Ridley will give him a pub of his own, but this expectation is dashed when it is discovered that the new Mrs Gee was once caught stealing from one of the brewery's pubs. Rita and Len, too old to adopt, foster children. Bert Tilsley is hurt in Brian's garage and later dies. Uncle Albert Tatlock also dies, followed soon afterwards by Stan Ogden. Bet becomes Queen of the Rovers. Gail and Brian split up but later get back together. Susan Barlow comes home after Tracey, upset, has run away to see her.

The Rovers burns to the ground in 1986. Bet is trapped inside but Kevin Webster rescues her. Ken sees red when Susan becomes engaged to his former rival Mike Baldwin. He shows up at the wedding just in time to give her away. Brian and Gail split up again over her affair with his Australian cousin, Ian and the birth of a baby girl, Sarah Louise. The baby is, in fact, Brian's and later they get back together.

In 1987 Bet at last marries wide boy Alec Gilroy and they run the Rovers together. Susan is pregnant but has an abortion and leaves Mike.

Tight Schedules, Trouble and Success

Coronation Street's complicated web of relationships, briefly hinted at above, is carefully plotted and executed by a talented team of professionals. Work on each show starts with a story conference the third Monday of every month. These meetings cover six episodes, or three weeks of transmission. The two story-line writers prepare the basic plots, then turn them over to some of the series' six writers, who are each commissioned to write a pair of episodes. These are prepared some three months in advance.

The Street's working week begins with exterior filming on Monday morning. Tuesday of each week is rehearsal day, from 10.30 a.m. to 5.30 p.m. The actors and director then join the crew for a technical run at 2.15 on Wednesdays, when shots are designed, camera motions run through, etc. The studio sets are finished on Wednesday night and actual taping is from 3 to 6.30 p.m. on Thursday and on Friday from 10 a.m. to 6.30 p.m. Shots are recorded out of sequence and carefully edited together to yield twenty-five minutes and thirty-five seconds of viewing pleasure, transmitted three weeks after recording.

Incidentally, there has been a shift of location since the early days. In the original permanent open air set, the houses were roughly two-thirds real size – mere shells supported by scaffolding. Only the railway viaduct was genuine. But a few years ago, because of the Manchester traffic scheme, the Street was pulled down and rebuilt on another site, with full-size houses. And there are also conducted tours inside the Rovers.

The series hasn't always had an easy run: in 1961 an actors' strike reduced the cast to thirteen, while footsteps and doors banging upstairs and offscreen implied the presence (or absence) of the other characters. The technicians' strike of 1979 succeeded in keeping the series off the air for eleven weeks, but only by shutting down the entire network! When the programme reappeared, Bet Lynch and Len Fairclough gave viewers an update, but the series suffered a major continuity gaffe anyway: summer-filmed episodes were already in the can when production started again in autumn. Back-

Stars of Coronation Street *held a party to celebrate the show's 21st birthday on 9th December 1981.*

to-back, these shows looked mighty peculiar – one week Ivy was saying how glorious summer was, and the next she was talking about Christmas! The Street's only other shutdown came in September 1986, when filming was suspended so that seventeen stars of the series could attend the New Orleans-style funeral of Pat Phoenix (Elsie Tanner) in Manchester.

The risky policy of live transmissions, standard procedure in television's salad days, has also made the Street bumpy at times. In the 1960s, *Coronation Street*'s first weekly episode would go out live, while the second would be tele-recorded, a process somewhere between taping and filming. The series' lack of editing meant mistakes and line fluffs went out live and uncorrected. However, an actor's ingenuity could always save the day: for example, in one corner shop scene, a heavy camera swooping in for a close-up on Pat Phoenix knocked over a display of tin cans. Watching them crash into

the camera's line of sight, Pat ad-libbed, 'Eh, I'll kill that bloody cat!'

Despite such difficulties, the programme has had an incredible history of success, cheered on by English viewers of every stripe. Sir John Betjeman once called *Coronation Street* the *Pickwick Papers* of the screen, adding, 'Not a word too many, not a gesture needless.' Russell Harty, Michael Parkinson and Willis Hall formed the British League for Hilda Ogden fans, while other boosters include Lord Olivier, Roy Orbison and Ella Fitzgerald.

There are *Coronation Street* appreciation societies at many British universities, including Cambridge. And rumours that the Queen watches dutifully were bolstered when she awarded Violet Carson (Ena Sharples) the OBE in 1965, Doris Speed (Annie Walker) the MBE in 1977 and Jack Howarth (Albert Tatlock) the MBE in 1983.

International Acclaim

The Aussies are great fans, having latched on to the programme via their Channel 9 network in 1963. Three years later Channel 9 requested a tour with at least three members of the cast. The lucky ambassadors chosen were Doris Speed (Annie Walker), Arthur Leslie (Jack Walker) and Pat Phoenix (Elsie Tanner), along with Granada executives Norman Frisby and H.V. Kershaw. Before leaving to meet flocks of thousands in Melbourne and Sydney, the stars were honoured with a special send-off at 10 Downing Street, a relaxed gathering presided over by Prime Minister Harold Wilson and his wife Mary, an ardent fan.

Perhaps the first British TV series to inspire fandom bordering on the fanatical, *Coronation Street* has inspired desperation in some viewers, eager for their weekly fix. A Dutch couple living on Great Barrier Island in New Zealand hooked their broken television to a 12-volt car battery to keep up with the Barlows et alia.

And at least one diehard fan resides in Monte Carlo – or did. Producer Bill Podmore received a letter from an English woman, employed as a millionaire's personal assistant in Monte Carlo. Though she made £12,000 a year, plus travel expenses

Violet Carson as the formidable Ena Sharples in a scene from Coronation Street *in 1961.*

Pat Phoenix as Elsie Tanner in court (in 1969) charged with stealing a dress from the shop where she worked.

and clothes, she was unhappy, because she could only watch *Coronation Street* one week in five while on her monthly holiday (!) in England. 'I don't suppose you could find me a job like the one I have now somewhere in the world that has *Coronation Street*,' she asked Podmore.

Ironically, Americans have failed to support the series during two brief US runs, in 1972 and 1982-3. Christopher Schemering's *Soap Opera Encyclopedia* says 'American audiences found the characters difficult to identify with.' More difficult than the Carringtons?

Of course, its cast has duly become famous, but some less regular actors have also shot to fame after their appearances on the series. Pop stars David Jones (The Monkees) and Peter Noone (Herman's

Hermits) both made early non-musical con-tributions, as Ena Sharples' grandson Colin Lomax and Len Fairclough's son Stanley, respectively. Angela Douglas, wife of the late Kenneth More, appeared as a girlfriend of Dennis Tanner, while Bill Maynard portrayed song agent Mickey Malone when Stan Ogden began stealing and selling Ena's tunes. Arthur Lowe, later a household name in *Dad's Army*, was featured as Leonard Swindley. Martin Shaw, of *The Professionals*

fame, appeared as a hippy in 1968, *Avengers* girl Joanna Lumley was a Ken Barlow girl-friend in 1973, and other guest turns include Max Wall, Stan Stenett and even Ben Kingsley!

Ratings Busters

Coronation Street has never had a problem attracting an audience, and indeed has tended to play down ratings-builders such as weddings rather than submerge them in media hype. Some of its story-lines, however, have drawn the nation's interest to an amazing degree. When Harry and Concepta Hewitt's baby son Christopher was kidnapped by Joan Akers and found by Elsie, the final episode of the drama drew 26 million viewers, and to this day holds the number four spot of the all-time most-viewed programmes in the UK.

Ninth place in that same list goes to the 1986 Rovers Return fire, caused by an electrical fault. Jack Duckworth rewired the pub's ancient electrical system, putting a heavy fuse in the fuse box, which conse-

In 1982 the Queen visited Coronation Street *and was intrigued by Bet's ear-rings.*

Linus Roache and Wendy Jane Walker played the parts of Ken Barlow's twin children.

quently exploded, setting the pub's cellar afire. As it spread, the blaze nearly claimed the life of Bet Lynch, and was watched by 22.75 million people. That, with 1.75 million more viewers, nudges the wedding of Charles and Diana into tenth place!

The Triangle That Shook Britain

Surprisingly, the top ten ratings list doesn't include one of the Street's most gripping storylines: the Deirdre/Mike/Ken affair, obsessively watched by millions of people. Deirdre Barlow (played by Anne Kirkbride) kept the nation gripped while she toyed with the idea of deserting Ken Barlow (William Roache) for the sexier, and certainly livelier Mike Baldwin (Johnny Briggs). Stories in the national press debated the outcome, and Noreen Taylor of the *Daily Mirror* (always the Street's friend, it seems), opined that the

show would never be the same again after such perfidy.

Backstage, William Roache tried a spot of method acting and kept the tension electric by refusing to speak to Johnny Briggs, going so far as to snub his fellow actor when Johnny greeted him with 'Good morning.'

While letters poured in to assuage Ken's feelings, Heineken produced an ad saying 'Try a pint, Ken, it might just work.' Whether Ken quaffed a keg or two we'll never know, but he must have tried something – in a burst of temper the normally noble and fair-minded Mr Barlow gave Deirdre a piece of his mind, and convinced her that she was married to a real man after all.

On the night her momentous decision to dump Mike was televised, Manchester United fans were away from their sets and watching a home game at Old Trafford. The score board flashed at half-time, 'DEIRDRE AND KEN BACK TOGETHER!' The stadium, like the country, sighed with relief.

Incidentally, Ken and Deirdre were married a mere two years earlier, in July 1981 – by a real preacher. Handling the task, a few days before Charles's royal wedding, was the Reverend Frank Topping, a real clergyman. If that ceremony was valid, are William Roache and Anne Kirkbride really married? No, answers Reverend Topping, but Ken and Deirdre really are!

Stars of the Street

Those viewers who urged Deirdre to go with Mike labelled Ken as dull, as did the press. One man who takes vociferous objection is William Roache, who portrays Ken. Like Ken, William has been married twice and though he regrets the decision to kill off his first screen wife, he claims that decision has made Ken a more thoughtful character, an emotional survivor.

William Roache's background included both military work and cinema parts when he returned north for the part of Ken Barlow on a show his agent assured him couldn't possibly last longer than its scheduled thirteen-week run. (The agent may have had a look at that original thirteenth episode script, replete with bulldozer.) William reluctantly accepted the role, which began on the series'

first episode. 'All I can say is it's been a long thirteen weeks,' says William today.

William is managed by his second wife, Sara, with whom he runs a theatrical production company. He recently suffered the tragic death of his eighteen-month-old daughter, Edwina, who succumbed to a viral infection. The couple have two other children, William and Verity. William golfs for relaxation, and played along top pro Sandy Lyle in the Benson and Hedges Pro Am. Competition.

Eileen Derbyshire has played on the Street almost as long as Barlow, having joined in 1961 as Emily Bishop, née Nugent. Eileen shares little in common with Emily – she enjoys family life, a small menagerie of pets, gardening and the theatre. She and her husband Thomas were married on 1 April soon after the show began – Eileen, holding to superstition, didn't get to the church before noon.

Before her son Oliver began university, she gave him a more normal, caring childhood than that experienced by many show-business children. She once delivered the newspaper to a shocked Stuart Hall, TV presenter, saying her son was on a school trip and would lose his round if no one stood in for him. A fan of Coronation Street, Oliver once told Eileen, 'Mum, I'm so glad you're in this, because if you weren't you would switch it off and tell me not to watch such rubbish!'

Thelma Barlow (no relation!) had played mostly in classical repertory theatre when she quit a secretarial job in Huddersfield to join a workshop at the Theatre Royal, Stratford East, under the command of innovative director Joan Littlewood. What is a classically trained actress doing playing dithery Mavis Riley? Says Thelma, 'I know she is a bit soggy but she is a sensible woman and nobody's fool, and never afraid to act on her principles.'

One of Thelma's favourite story-lines had Mavis stalked by two suitors, Derek Wilton and Victor Pendlebury. The saga of Derek the drip, Victor the vamp and Mave the rave began when Mavis left Derek to go on a chaste camping trip with Victor, whom she had met at an evening art class. Derek settled the matter by proposing, but on the wedding

Eileen Derbyshire (Emily Bishop), Julie Goodyear (Bet Lynch) and Thelma Barlow (Mavis Riley).

day, neither Derek nor Mavis showed up! Derek latter married another woman, but still sees unmarried Mavis.

In 1966, a former model and walk-on actress changed the face of *Coronation Street*. Julie Goodyear, appearing in the Granada series *A Family at War*, was asked by its producer June Howson to play a small part in the new series she was about to bring out as one of the girls in the old raincoat factory on the Street. Julie's ingenious rendition of Bet Lynch made the character a series staple.

Soapmania has made Julie's life almost as public as Bet's. The press has dwelt on the divorce that ended her third marriage, her love life, her nervous breakdown, a very damaging court case and her operation for cervical cancer, which caused her to take six weeks off the series. Only seventeen when her son Gary was born, she raised him in a flat over the pub her mother ran, and sold vacuum cleaners and speedboats before her career took off.

Despite such 'scandalous' details, Julie has always been one of Britain's favourite television actresses, and has been the subject of a *This is Your Life*, where she cried when meeting the nun who nursed her during her cancer operation. Bet too is a fan's delight, and was made landlady of the Rovers Return in 1985, taking over from Annie Walker. In April 1987 Julie left the series for a few months to care for her sick mother, Alice, who died soon afterwards. Bet returned in September to reign at the Rovers again, restoring her and Julie's special charm to the Street.

The Street's other cult heroine is Hilda Ogden, who, with her lazy spouse Stan, created one of the medium's most memorable married couples. Tough, nosy and never at a loss, Hilda was brought to life by Jean Alexander, ensuring the actress a place in TV's hall of fame. Indeed, Jean has been voted the fourth most popular female in Britain,

23

Johnny Briggs (Mike Baldwin) and William Roache (Ken Barlow) with their wives.

Jean Alexander in her Hilda Ogden mac.

trailing only the Queen, Queen Mother and Princess of Wales!

Britain loves a scrapper, and the Garrick Club's elite of the theatrical world have formed a Hilda Ogden Appreciation Society, one of many in the country. Hilda was a survivor, as witnessed by probably her most moving scene, when told of the death of her husband, Stan. A model of restraint, Jean based Hilda's response on her mother's grief when Jean's father died. 'I knew Hilda would never let anyone see her cry,' says Jean. 'She'd keep her pecker up.'

Originally a trained librarian, Jean later joined the Adelphi Guild Theatre, took elocution lessons to soften her Liverpool accent, and spent many years in rep before taking roles in *Z Cars* and *Television Club*. A sensitive, talented actress, Jean sees herself as Hilda's opposite, and even told a woman's magazine that she was still a virgin at sixty (true or not, it's a claim Hilda would never make). Still, Jean has a firm grasp of her character's personality. 'She reminds me of one of those unsinkable ducks you float in the bath,' Jean says. 'No matter how many times she gets pushed under she'll still bob back for more. There's no holding Hilda down!'

Indeed, the only person who could best Hilda is Jean Alexander herself. In mid-1987, the actress announced that, having passed sixty, she would not renew her contract with the series. Pressure from the many pro-Hilda organisations, including Granada TV, may bring her out of retirement for welcome guest appearances.

A boy actor and singer, Johnny Briggs got an early start in show business, singing in *La Bohème* at the Cambridge Theatre in 1947. He starred as Det. Sgt. Russell in *No Hiding Place* in the mid-1960s, and made an appearance a few years later in *Crossroads*. In 1976 he had just finished a film, *Au Pair*, and a play at the Royal Court when he was approached to do *Coronation Street*. Wary about signing a long-term contract, he was told he would only have a three-month affair with Bet Lynch. He stayed in the role of Mike Baldwin, however, first as a romeo and now as a settled Londoner. Each year the actor helps promote the Johnny Briggs charity golf match.

Mike's wedding was one of the most controversial in the Street's history. The huge age gap between him and Susan Barlow, Ken's daughter, provoked the father's disapproval. Ken, of course, already had reason enough to dislike Mike, and this marriage fuelled his outraged fire.

Anne Kirkbride began on the Street as Deirdre Langton, and almost ended that way too. When Ray Langton headed for Holland with another woman, the producers felt that Deirdre should disappear. Anne argued that the series could show the travails of a single parent, and saved her character. Now, of course, she's Deirdre Barlow, married to Ken, who shares Anne's interest in astrology. The Street's producers spotted her in Granada's television play *Another Sunday and Sweet FA* as Shirley, the girlfriend of a Sunday league footballer, and recruited her.

As Gail Tilsley, Helen Worth has enjoyed some of the best scenes of the series. The breakup of her marriage to Brian, their reunion and the subsequent divorce over Sarah Louise, thought to be Brian's cousin's child, all proved that the soaps could provide gripping entertainment. Helen is in her second decade with *Coronation Street*, and earlier appeared on *Z Cars* and *Dr Who*. Her infectious laugh marks a warm and giving person; she helped colleague Jill Summers cope with the death of her husband Clifford several years ago.

Another actor to receive choice moments is Bryan Mosley, who plays corner shop owner Alf Roberts. Bryan popped in and out of the cast from 1961 to 1968, when he became a regular. Alf's wife Renee was later killed in a car crash and Alf himself was injured when a lorry crashed into the Rovers Return – Bryan received letters inquiring after Alf's health, and even offering him a convalescence stay at a hotel. Bryan's own life has also had dangerous episodes: while

Helen Worth (Gail Tilsley) with actor Mike Angelis.

on safari in Africa with his wife, Norma, he was charged by two lions, but by keeping cool managed to keep the beasts at bay.

Michael Le Vell's moment of peril came while actually playing his role, mechanic Kevin Webster. In rescuing Bet Lynch from the Rovers fire in June 1986, Michael developed a chest condition from the fumes spewed by the flames and the smoke canisters. Michael, who had parts at Oldham Rep and worked on other Granada TV productions before the Street, recently married Janette Beverley, who starred in the BBC's *Sharon and Elsie*. At about the same time, Kevin married Sally Seddon.

Actor Michael Le Vell (Kevin Webster) marries his true-life sweetheart Janette Beverley.

For her part actress Sally Whittaker had an inglorious start to the series, thanks to Michael Le Vell. Kevin and Sally Seddon met when he accidentally splashed dirty water over her. This was Sally Whittaker's first scene for the series and she was told there would be no rehearsal. While she stood on a chilly Manchester kerb in the morning, Michael, as Kevin, drove his car too far forward and doused Sally from head to toe with filthy water. In fact, Michael didn't get the splashing correct until the third take.

Motherly barmaid Betty Turpin is played both by a Betty and an ex-bar owner, Betty Driver, who once ran a pub for five years with her sister Freda. Betty claims their pub, in Cheshire, was haunted: glasses vibrated for no reason, bar shelves gave off weird noises, and both plants and aquarium fish died *en masse*. After such hair-raising experiences, the drunken Rovers revellers are a piece of cake.

Another barmaid, blonde bombshell Gloria Todd, poured drinks for six episodes in 1984 and turned enough heads to be invited back full-time in June 1985. Soon after rejoining the cast, actress Sue Jenkins became pregnant (by her husband David Fleshman, of *Boys from the Blackstuff*). The Rovers bar hid Sue's pregnancy until a few weeks before the birth, and after little Emily Victoria was born, Gloria reappeared behind the bar.

For a time, loud-mouthed Vera Duckworth dominated Liz Dawn – when the actress was invited to open a school fête or participate in a cabaret the punters wanted Vera, not Liz. Her fame and the stress that accompanied it put a strain on her marriage and caused problems at work. But when Liz's father died, a change came over her; she stopped smoking, stopped drinking, lost weight and got back with her husband. Liz is now in fine form to continue donning a wig and sounding off as Vera.

Vera's husband Jack is also known for his voice, in particular his notoriously bad singing. Indeed, Jack's cacophonous croaking in one episode actually lost actor William Tarmey bookings in night clubs – the owners feared William was as off-key as Jack. William has recently taken time off the series to have a life-saving heart operation.

In 1979 a new family moved into number 5 Coronation Street – the Tilsleys.

Like William, Sue Nicholls sings professionally and has even appeared on *Top of the Pops*, something character Audrey Roberts could never aspire to. The TOTP break came in 1968 when Sue, as waitress Marilyn Gates, sang, 'Where Will You Be When I Need You?' on *Crossroads*. Released as a single, it got to number seventeen and stayed in the charts for eight weeks. Sue is actually the Honourable Susan Frances Harmer Nicholls, being the daughter of Lord and Lady Harmer Nicholls of Staffordshire. She shares her life with fellow Street actor Mark Eden (Allan Bradley).

Ivy Tilsley is played by impulse buyer Lynne Perrie, who own six television sets and a wardrobe full of madcap purchases! Actually, they're not that mad – after buying a knitting machine, Lynne learned how to use it professionally. She has also crocheted a suit for Julie Goodyear over four years.

Her son on the series, Brian, is played by heart-throb Chris Quinten, who appears in the national dailies and teen magazines as a pin-up, TV star and football player. Chris plays football for the Street's all-star's team, and played in a celebrity match at the 1987 Cup Final.

True Believers
With such a popular programme, the thin line between reality and telefantasy is often erased. For example, a trio of girls once wrote to the producers, asking if they could get jobs together in Mike Baldwin's factory, saying that 'We have worked together since leaving school, and would like to continue to do so.' In another incident, a marriage bureau in the Midlands offered its services to

27

Bet Lynch, claiming it could find her a husband.

Everyone's favourite pub, the Rovers Return, is the focus of much attention and confusion. Around November each year the production staff begins getting requests to book the pub for office parties. Temperance societies are quite alarmed at the prodigious amounts of liquor that flow inside. Even the experts can be fooled – a licensee from Gilford once wrote to ask how they had time to film in the Rovers Return between licensing hours.

Still the King

Coronation Street has always been one of the top ITV programmes, despite the BBC's attempts to dim its bulb by placing opposite it such highly ranked series as *Steptoe and Son* and *Till Death Do Us Part*. In fact, the only slippage of the Street has been caused by the sudden popularity of other soaps, notably *Crossroads* in the mid-1970s, and, since 1985, *EastEnders*. The latter has put the squeeze on *Coronation Street*'s soap supremacy, but to those who recall the golden moments of the Street's 28-year history, there is still only one king.

Coronation Street's 25th birthday in 1985.

Coronation Street

First episode credits:
Transmitted 9 December, 1960
Produced by Stuart Latham
Created by Tony Warren
A Granada TV Production

Original Cast List

Character	*Actor*
Mrs Lappin	Maudie Edwards
Florrie Lindley	Betty Alberge
Linda Cheveski	Anne Cunningham
Elsie Tanner	Patricia Phoenix
Dennis Tanner	Philip Lowrie
Kenneth Barlow	William Roache
Ida Barlow	Noel Dyson
Frank Barlow	Frank Pemberton
David Barlow	Alan Rothwell
Ena Sharples	Violet Carson
Albert Tatlock	Jack Howarth
Susan Cunningham	Patricia Shakesby
Annie Walker	Doris Speed

3
Crossroads –
Room at the Inn

For lovers of popular culture, 1964 is chiefly remembered as the year Beatlemania kicked into high gear, launching the 'British invasion' in America and spurring waves of fringed teens to clutch jangling electric guitars. In a quieter way, 1964 also made soap opera history, as it saw the birth of the UK's first daily serial, *Crossroads*.

The idea of a daily serial had been kicking around ATV since 1958. ATV's Reg Watson, an Australian, had told ATV boss Sir Lew Grade how impressed he was with the live daily serials in the USA. Watson waited six years for a reply, but when he got one it was definite: Grade asked him to produce a daily serial for ATV called *Midland Road*, written by Peter Ling and Hazel Adair.

Watson agreed and, after a local competition which changed the name to *Crossroads*, casting began. Noele Gordon, hostess of a programme Watson produced called *Lunch Box*, was selected for the pivotal role of Meg Richardson. Throngs of young actors from all over the country interviewed for the part of her son Sandy, but no one seemed right until Roger Tonge, accidentally sent into a high-level *Crossroads* meeting by a cleaning woman, caught the directors' eyes. Meg's daughter Jill was another tough search solved by accident – Jane Rossington, waiting for an audition, burst into the casting offices screaming she'd missed her train and landed the role.

Meg and her family were the linchpins of the serial. The story revolved around the newly opened *Crossroads* motel in King's Oak, just outside Birmingham. The inn was run by Meg Richardson with the help of her family. Most of the drama from the first episodes would involve Meg and her children – Sandy and his school friend Colin breaking into the nearby hotel, Fairlawns, to switch the sugar and salt (and getting caught), Sandy developing a crush on Colin's sister – as well as the other Richardson relatives.

With these crucial parts cast, Watson turned to production details. The music, commissioned from Tony Hatch, remained throughout most of the series' run. Less successful were the Alpha television studios used by ATV in Aston, Birmingham. The building, a former cinema and theatre, accommodated only tight sets and cramped crew set-ups, but the *Crossroads* staff had to make do.

Crossroads Critics and Chaos

From its debut on 2 November 1964 at 6.30 p.m., *Crossroads* was an instant success, at least with the restricted section of the public privileged to see it, for it was some eight years before it went country-wide. Not everyone at ATV agreed, largely due to the slapdash elements that accrue to daily serials. Bill Ward, production chief at ATV, chafed at media putdowns and unfavourable comparisons with *Emergency Ward 10*, ATV's big-budget soap. Thinking that one bad apple made ATV's output look a bit rotten, he

Hazel Adair and Peter Ling – Crossroads *creators.*

Paul Henry who plays Benny.

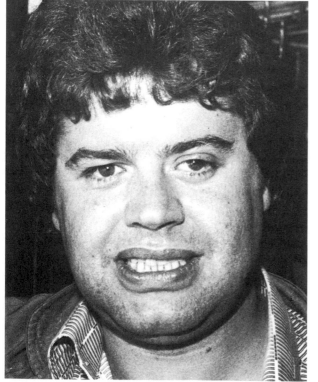

campaigned to kill the series, but was over-ruled by Sir Lew Grade.

Following its smooth beginning, the series has taken its bumps, due in general to what Bill Ward found objectionable, its almost amateurish quality. After the series was cut from five days to four, the IBA (Independent Broadcasting Authority) protested its continued weaknesses, and in 1980 said the series would have to be cut to three days unless its scripts and acting improved. They did, at least enough to pacify the IBA.

'It's more interesting watching paint dry,' quipped comedian Jasper Carrott about *Crossroads*, echoing sentiments that have flitted across the newpapers' review columns from time to time. Radio Rentals even produced an ad for a video machine that read, 'It can take sixteen episodes of Cross-roads (if you can!)' But when one daily called the show amateurish around its fifteenth anniversary in 1979, Noele Gordon responded by saying, 'If used in the proper context, "amateur" means "for the love of". We are very proud to be amateurs in that sense.'

Certainly love sometimes seemed to be the only thing holding the series together, as viewers were asked in their fondness to excuse bizarre lapses in logic. In 1980, both the kitchens and chef Shughie McFee just disappeared, never to be seen again – due to lack of studio space. Presumably, service at the motel declined, though no guests complained. Also MIC once (Missing in *Crossroads*) was the lovable halfwit Benny. Sent off for a spanner while working in the motel's garage, Benny vanished for six months without a word from the other characters. Now, we know Benny's slow, but . . .

Hasty filming and seat-of-the-pants production also made *Crossroads* infamous for on-screen goofs. One victim was Jane Rossington (Jill), called upon to play a particular scene with a Great Dane. The dog idly lapped its paws until Jane took the leash and the director shouted 'Action!' At this point the animal went wild and dragged Jane through the motel door, which viewers were supposed to believe had glass in it. The scene was, of course, shot live.

But enough carps. The series did last 23 years, racking up fans until the end, and along the way adding to the soap mythos many captivating story-lines, touching scenes and enchanting characters.

The Motel's Story, 1964–88

The Crossroads motel opens in 1964, run by Meg Richardson. She must immediately cope with staff crises, such as when Chef Vi Blundell objects to Carlos Rafael, a Spanish cook. Classy Meg has a heart of gold, and fosters Stevie Harris, a young girl rejected by her mother. Meg's son Sandy, meanwhile, is accused of stealing from the rival hotel, Fairlawns. He later goes on a school trip to Paris.

Meg soon meets Hugh Mortimer, a local businessman, and the two fall in love. Lightning strikes in 1967 when workmen at the motel trigger off an old war bomb. While reconstruction goes on at the demolished Crossroads, Meg takes some of her staff to Tunisia to help friends open a hotel there.

When Meg knocks local postman Vince Parker off his motorbike, she spends a month in jail for dangerous driving. Hugh Mortimer marries another woman, Jane Templeton, and Meg marries Malcolm Ryder. Heavily in debt, Malcolm insures Meg and tries to poison her to cash in on the policy. When their housekeeper warns Meg, Malcolm flees to South America, and is later rumoured to have died in a car crash. Meg's pregnant daughter Jill has her own marital problems: after wedding motel manager John Crane, she learns he's a bigamist, and the shock causes her to miscarry.

After Diane marries postman Vince Parker, her illegitimate son Nickie is kidnapped by his pop-star father and taken to the USA. Jill marries Stan Harvey. Sandy Richardson is crippled and confined to a wheelchair after a car crash. David Hunter joins the motel staff. In 1975, Hugh Mortimer returns with plans to wed Meg, but is stalled by Malcolm Ryder's return. Malcolm is arrested for Meg's attempted murder. Hugh and Meg marry at last.

In 1977, a simpleton named Benny makes his first appearance, with Miss Diane on her Uncle Ed's farm. Benny's girlfriend, a gypsy named Maureen Flynn, is killed. Soon thereafter, Benny is accused and then cleared of murdering Linda Welch, the sister of a girl he has offered to marry though she is pregnant by someone else.

Jill's stormy marital career continues to rock as she bears a boy, Matthew, by her stepbrother Anthony Mortimer. Matthew is taken away to New York, Stan Harvey leaves and Jill seeks refuge in drugs. Tragedy hits Meg, too, as Hugh is kidnapped by a terrorist and dies of a heart attack. David Hunter's son Chris is involved in the crime. David himself is shot by his ex-wife Rosemary, but later marries novelist Barbara Brady.

The motel burns down in 1981. Meg is thought to be inside, but in fact the only fatality is Sam Hurst, a friend of Benny's. Meg sails off on the QE2 for a new life.

Arthur Brownlow is killed in a hit-and-run car accident by a drunken motel guest.

Jill marries Adam Chance, and Meg reappears on their honeymoon in Venice. When an international hotel chain buys out Crossroads, the Hunters leave but Jill and Adam stay. Glamorous new boss Nicola Freeman redesigns the motel. However, Miranda Pollard is raped soon afterwards by a motel guest, and Mr Paul, the *maître de* at the restaurant, is attacked when he tries to stop a wages snatch.

More bad news for Jill: after her affair with Mickey, Nicola's brother, her marriage to Adam breaks up. Jill loses the baby she wanted so much.

The new year of 1987 is rung in with another ownership change, as Nicola Freeman's company sells the motel to local steak bar owner Tommy (Bomber) Lancaster. He changes the name to Crossroads Country Hotel. Miss Diane dies of a brain haemorrhage. In her honour, Benny pays for a donkey's keep and calls the animal Miss Diane. The Grice family buy the village shop, but their lease is short-lived: the series ends in March 1988.

Ahead of its Time

Although a 'teatime' soap, *Crossroads* plots broke new ground for soap operas, as when Sandy Richardson's car accident forced him to spend the rest of his life in a wheelchair. This was the first time a disabled person figured so prominently in a British TV series, and it led to the formation of a *Crossroads* Care Scheme, which helps families of disabled people by providing care attendants who relieve stress.

Crossroads also became the first series to feature a Down's Syndrome child, in a 1983 story-line that showed the problems of a mother caring for such a child. The story-line, which won acclaim from viewers and press, featured actress Nina Weill, herself afflicted with Down's Syndrome.

New levels of excitement were reached with the series. The first big *Crossroads* cliff-hanger came in 1967, when workmen at the motel found and accidentally triggered off an

(l to r) Sue Nicolls, Lew Luton, Noele Gordon and Tony Merton.

Previous page *Gabrielle Drake of Crossroads – the press called her the 'new' Meg.*
Above *That famous woolly hat – Benny and dog Moses.*
Below *Sue Hanson who plays 'Miss Diane'.*

1975: the happy couple, Hugh and Meg, alias John Bentley and Noele Gordon.

old war time-bomb. The explosion shattered much of the existing motel – which is just what the producers wanted, as they were moving to new studios and needed an excuse to show new sets.

The next *Crossroads* cliffhanger took place entirely off-screen. When Thames TV took over the London area franchise from Rediffusion, it pulled *Crossroads* off the air and put on its own series. London audiences were up in arms at this affront, and after six months of impassioned debate, including an intercession from Mary Wilson, the Prime Minister's wife, *Crossroads* reopened in London.

(Of course, this meant *Crossroads* was six months behind in London, compared with the rest of the country – certainly a rare situation. An hour-long special in 1975 brought the slowpokes up-to-date in time for Meg's wedding.)

Also in the 1960s, Meg spent a month in jail for dangerous driving. This message-oriented story-line depended on accuracy, as its aim was to show how respectable people unexpectedly land in trouble. The production team took expert advice to ensure the court and prison scenes looked authentic.

ATV also based its prison sets on Winson Green men's prison for the two weeks Meg ended up in jail.

From the time Meg landed in the pen, anguished viewers lit up the switchboard – not at ATV, but at Winson Green. Callers asked about visiting hours and whether flowers and gifts could be delivered. ATV was forced to give Winson Green a special number that linked callers back to ATV, where switchboard operators spent two weeks fielding distressed people on the 'Meg line'.

(Incidentally, the change from ATV to Central TV took place at the start of 1982, when the franchise for the Midlands went from the first company to the second.)

Meg's wedding in 1975 brought the series to its height of popularity – a level which, sadly, it never regained. Her marriage to Hugh Mortimer (John Bentley) was filmed over two days in the programme's first real extravaganza, which featured much previously unheard-of outside filming.

33

Somehow, before the outside shots at a Birmingham registry office, St Philip's Cathedral in Birmingham and the Droitwich Hotel in the Warwickshire countryside, the press had learned (and, of course, leaked) the filming dates.

Thousands of viewers flocked to the cathedral to watch Meg and Hugh tie the knot, and the massed hordes brought the centre of Birmingham to a standstill. The crowds' presence, however, visible in the background of the wedding scenes, was never explained to the series' viewers. Exactly why thousands of people would throng to watch a small-time motel owner marry a businessman was left to the imagination. Maybe no one wondered; the event had taken on such momentous significance to media-followers that the huddled onlookers seemed as natural as they would at a royal wedding. Indeed, the *TV Times* even produced a *Crossroads* wedding souvenir at 35p with colour photos of the wedding.

Goodbye, Meg

Six years later, Meg figured in the most controversial occurrence in *Crossroads*' history, an event that eclipsed her wedding and prefigured the series' cancellation six years later. To an unprecedented hype-storm and an angry barrage of protests from viewers, Meg Richardson Mortimer vanished from *Crossroads* in 1981.

Almost as shocking was the reason behind it: Meg had to go because Noele Gordon had been sacked. In 1981, Jack Barton, who had taken over as producer from Reg Watson in 1972, handed Noele her notice. The dismissal made national news headlines and was covered by both BBC and ITV nightly news. The reason for the decision has never been satisfactorily explained, and Noele herself claimed not to know.

Once the news of Meg's imminent departure broke, speculation flourished as to how she would meet her end. Most people assumed she would die, and indeed Barton, to outwit the press, filmed multiple final bows for Meg, including death by fire in a motel catastrophe and death by drug overdose. Grieving fans, led by future *That's Life* presenter Bill Buckley, started a 'Meg is Magic' campaign. Hundreds protested out-

The cast of Crossroads.

side ATV's studios with banners, and there was even a 'Meg is Magic' record. The *Daily Star* joined the fight with a 'Save our Meg' rally.

Though she didn't die, she did disappear. On 5 November 1981, seventeen years to the week since the series premiered, the *Crossroads* motel did burn down, but Meg lived through the fire. She departed for New York on the QE2 and returned briefly to rendez-vous with Jill on the latter's honeymoon in Venice in 1983. Noele Gordon, for so long the cornerstone of *Crossroads*, died in 1985.

The Producers They Are A'Changing

Besides prompting Meg to leave for New York, the motel blaze enabled Barton to remodel, as the bomb had done for Watson, and he sought a real hotel that could serve as a model. He found the Golden Valley Hotel outside Cheltenham, a four-star establishment whose exterior served for *Crossroads'* outside filming. The sets built on the Golden Valley plan were larger and looked better on television.

It seems to have been a *Crossroads* producer's prerogative to change the sets: the first thing Philip Bowman did when he took the helm in 1984 was to build more colourful reception and other areas and to switch outside filming to the Penns Hall Hotel in Sutton Coldfield. Since the series' original premise states that the motel was built on the grounds of an old Victorian house, Penns Hotel looked the part. Viewers seemed happy with the change, and Bowman never felt the need to explain the change via a script wherein the old (well, three years old) motel was nuked or eaten by termites.

Less popular was Bowman's decision to remodel the cast, chiefly by sacking four actors and writing out their very major characters. Barbara and David Hunter, played by

35

Sue Lloyd and Ronnie Allen, and Glenda and Kevin Banks, played by Lynette McMorrough and David Moran, were replaced by lots of new characters. Bowman, who was criticised for what many saw as a ruthless elimination of good characters, responded by saying, 'It was very difficult to change the cast and the sets.'

A mere eighteen months later, Bowman himself was gone, as former *Archers* producer William Smethurst took over the series. He fired more of the cast, including Sue Hanson, who had played Miss Diane for twenty years. Besides the elimination of Meg Richardson, this was the sharpest casting blow dealt the series. But drastic measures are often necessitated by drastic situations, and observers deduced that *Crossroads* was in trouble, more trouble than another change of sets would solve. Within two years they would learn how right they were.

Staff, Guests and Friends
Noele Gordon, Roger Tonge and a few other *Crossroads* actors appear in the Gone But Not Forgotten chapter. With *Crossroads*' cancellation, the rest of the cast described below are now also 'gone', but for quite different reasons.

Had the series lasted, it's a safe bet that Jane Rossington would have been in it. The only member of the original cast to last until the final shutdown, Rossington, as Jill Richardson, spoke the first ever words on *Crossroads*, 'Crossroads motel, may I help you?' Midlands born and bred, she trained at the Rose Bradford School of Speech and Drama. When she left, she landed the role of Kate Ford, a probationer nurse, in ATV's bigger-budgeted soap *Emergency Ward 10*. After stage roles, Jane came to the *Crossroads* cast. Even after joining, she would take breaks to appear in stage and TV productions, and made an appearance on BBC's radio soap *The Archers*.

Jane and Jill became pregnant at the same time, so Jill's on-screen heaviness was not padding. Jill's baby, Sarah Jane, was also played by Jane's daughter Sorrel, last seen as a bridesmaid at Jill's wedding (not Jane's – she was already happily married to chartered surveyor David Dinger).

Jill and Adam Chance (Jane Rossington and Tony Adam).

A shocking scene for Jane occurred when she filmed a dialogue in bed with Jill's lover Mickey Doyle, played by Martin Smith. Martin wore his pants in rehearsal, but slyly stripped them off beneath the covers when the cameras started to roll. When Jane saw what the camera couldn't, she screamed, and then fell about laughing with Martin. 'I'll never forget the scene,' she says. 'It was 9 a.m.!'

When asked why she stuck with the show for so long, Jane replied that she read reports in the press that the show was to stop. So, she figured, she might as well stay on until it finished. And she did – though the reports she was referring to were published in the 1960s!

Paul Henry, another Midlander, spent eight years with the Birmingham Repertory Theatre, appearing in such productions as *Romeo and Juliet*, *Othello*, *The Merchant of Venice*, *Investigation*, *The Recruiting Officer* and *Dandy Dick*. He also featured in BBC versions of *Romeo and Juliet* and *A Midsummer Night's Dream* and Thames TV's *The Sweeney*, and got his first soap taste in *The Archers*. Little did he dream his dramatic talent would later be channelled into playing a halfwit in a silly hat!

As Benny Hawkins, Paul found lasting fame, including a treasured episode of *This Is Your Life* – he says of his wife Sheila, who lured him to the show, 'I'll never trust her again!' Paul has two children, Justine and Anthony, and often performs in sell-out pantomime seasons. Lucky attendees even get to purchase official Benny hats!

Poor Benny has always been a fan favourite, and sympathetic viewers will brook no mistreatment of the simple soul. The greatest support from his adoring audience came when Benny was accused of murdering Linda Welch. Of course, Benny didn't do it – he merely found Linda's body. She had hit her head on the sink and died after being pushed by garage manager Colin Dutton. Dutton blamed Benny, and during the police investigation fans mounted a 'Benny Is Innocent' protest and blocked studio switchboards! Dutton later confessed to the accidental murder.

As Miss Diane, Sue Hanson enjoyed some twenty-two years on the series until her un-

Ann George (Amy Turtle) returns to the series.

timely, and unstylish, write-out in spring 1987. After Sue's row with the Smethurst administration over money, Miss Diane suffered a quick brain haemorrhage, lay in a hospital bed for two weeks and then passed away. As Sue notes, the funeral scenes cost more than her death scenes. When she passed away, viewers flooded Central's switchboard with bereaved calls, and operators said many callers were in tears.

Sue's acting experience ranged from the Bristol Old Vic to TV appearances with the Dave Clark Five. She is married to pop star Carl Wayne of The Move and has a young son Jack. Her bitterness about the way she left *Crossroads* stems from the fun she had doing what she considered a fairly light-weight show. When the motel burnt down in 1981, Sue and the other cast repeatedly burst into scene-destroying laughter as Miss Diane was forced to intone seriously, 'The switchboard is in ashes.'

When producer Bill Smethurst took over, one of the 'new' characters he introduced was old-timer Amy Turtle, played by Ann George, whose earlier stint on the show ran

(Above) *Dee Hepburn (Anne-Marie Wade).*
(Left) *Terence Rigby (Tommy Lancaster)*

from 1965 to 1975. Ann was never given any reason for her termination, but it may have something to do with her uncanny ability to forget her lines – this endeared her to bemused fans, but not to the producers. Still, she had good reason to bridle at the way she was dismissed: an ATV make-up girl just told her to clear out her dressing room.

Ann made her first stage appearance at the tender age of four, and was for years a noted singer with the D'Oyly Carte. She treasured her days on *Crossroads*, and jumped at the chance to return in 1987, though only for guest appearances. When she walked on to the set for the first time in ten years, the performers and crew applauded, bringing tears to her eyes.

Do you believe in ghosts? Tony Adams didn't – until the *Crossroads* actor began sensing the presence of his good friend Noele Gordon, who had died in 1985. The strange feelings intensified until, feeling Noele's spirit very strongly outside the *Crossroads* rehearsal room, Tony said, 'Hello, darling'. He consulted a spiritualist soon after that, who told him Noele wasn't totally at peace. In another peculiar experience, a wardrobe mistress gave him a message to buy some royal jelly. The wardrobe woman 'described Nolly to a T,' says Tony.

As motel smoothie Adam Chance, Tony was on his third soap role and his second in the series. In 1968 he played an estate agent who sold Meg's sister Kitty's house, and he has also played Dr Bywalters in ATV's *General Hospital*. An ardent sea lover, Tony has a 140-ton launch boat called *Kevalam*, which he hires out at £1,000 a day. He'd love to play in *Howard's Way* or to feature in a sea soap. None of this is any surprise to family friends – Tony's mother, Winifred Brown, was a famous sailor, pilot, explorer and sportswoman.

Besides the seaman, Tony Adams has a good deal of the practical joker in him. One of his favourite tricks before he quit *Crossroads* was to shock the extras who lug cases in and out of reception. These cases were empty props, at least until Tony got to them: between takes he'd load the cases with the heavy stage weights that hold the set down. His victims would have to tote the luggage anyway or risk ruining a take, which explains the pained expressions they often had.

A new face for Philip Bowman's 1980s *Crossroads*, Dee Hepburn was familiar as the athletic dream-date in Bill Forsyth's *Gregory's Girl*. Dee, from East Kilbride, quickly became one of the most popular new stars, but her first day on the set was a nightmare. The stress seemed to have been too much, as the young actress passed out behind the *Crossroads* reception desk and slept for two hours in the sick bay while her scenes were rescheduled. Nothing like making a good impression the first day!

Can you see nasty Tommy 'Bomber' Lancaster calling 'Out!' from the sidelines at Wimbledon? You may some day – actor Terence Rigby loves tennis so much he only accepted the part on condition he would get

Stan Stennett who played Sid Hooper.

time off for Wimbledon. He has passed his examination for the British Tennis Umpires Association and hopes to officiate one day. His screen wife Mary was played by Frances Cuka, a former RSC actor who came to the role from New York's production of *Nicholas Nickleby*. Former star of *The Archers* Kathryn Hurlbutt plays the part of his daughter.

Stan Stennett was so involved in his role as Sid Hooper that he became emotionally distraught by the scenes when Mavis, his screen wife, lay on her death bed. Stan, who was axed from the show early in 1987, once caused a considerable stir by asking Birmingham Council to provide him with a flat near the studios.

Behind sexy Fiona Harding is an actress with a will – Caroline Evans objected to a poolside scene that had her lounging in a wet swimsuit, and wanted to quit. The producers managed to talk her into staying until the show's finale. One tender bedroom scene between her and Fiona's lover Daniel Freeman (Philip Goodhew) ended in tears – his. Meant to nudge him in the chest, Caroline misjudged and smacked him in the groin. Unlucky Philip doubled up in pain, at which point Caroline accidentally struck him in the teeth!

Patrick Jordan, who plays doorman Mr Darby, barely made it to the series. In 1943, in North Africa, he took a shot in his left eye and hovered on the operating table between this world and the next. So precarious was his situation that the military command got the outcome wrong for a time – years later a platoon officer bumped into Patrick with considerable surprise, having already attended his funeral! Patrick has been married to book illustrator Margery Gill for more than forty years.

One of the hazards of being brought on to a series where stars have been fired is incurring the wrath of viewers. Many never forgave the Grice family for taking over the King's Oak shop, but the five-member household stuck it out anyway. Mother Margaret Grice had to look so plain that Meryl Hampton isn't allowed to wear any make-up on the show. Father Ray was played by Al Ashton, who's nothing like the layabout he portrayed. Al has written scripts for *Casualty* and *EastEnders*, including the episode when Michelle's baby was born. Rebellious Beverly was actually bubbly and high-spirited Karen Murden, aged seventeen, while Simon Love, who beat out 8,000 young hopefuls to play her TV brother, was only thirteen and still in school during the series. Soap fans may remember Grandma as actress Margaret Stallard, who has been in *Emmerdale Farm*.

One of the hits of the Smethurst season was Graham Seed, playing motel assistant manager Charlie Mycroft. Graham played upper-class twit Nigel Pargetter in *The Archers*.

The Curtain Falls

Viewers had hardly had time to get used to producer Philip Bowman before William Smethurst arrived with his cast changes. Mistrust of Smethurst was fuelled when a *Crossroads* script, allegedly found in a rubbish bin, indicated that more cast cuts were to come. Smethurst, calling this industrial espionage, was dubbed 'Barmy Bill' by *Sunday People* TV critic Margaret Forward.

In fact, Smethurst was trying hard to save the series. He saw himself as a surgeon carry-ing out delicate open-heart surgery on a dying patient. When it was announced in July 1987 that the series would end for good in April 1988, many blamed Smethurst, but Central admits that *Crossroads* had been dying a slow death for years, hence the multiple facelifts and producer changes.

Its death throes took an unexpected turn on 7 September 1987, when a final 'new look' *Crossroads* debuted. Planned months before the series was cancelled, the changes to the series were intended to draw new viewers. But the new music by Max Early and Raf Ravenscroft, new opening titles and new producer (Michele Buck, with Smethurst, now the executive producer) were too little, too late. Despite Central TV's efforts to save the series, these changes merely confused audiences who knew *Crossroads* had been cancelled.

Why did such a popular and long-lived series die? While the news stunned viewers, many see it as inevitable, and some suggest that the first seeds of doom were planted in 1981. *Crossroads* the motel was a dream of Meg Richardson. No young faces or new characters could make up for her loss. Without Meg, the motel and the series went on, but the dream was over.

Crossroads

First episode credits:
Transmitted 2 November, 1964
Produced by Reg Watson
Created by Hazel Adair and Peter Ling
An ATV Production

Original Cast List

Character	Actor
Jill Richardson	Jane Rossington
Frank Gillow	Alan Haywood
Meg Richardson	Noele Gordon
Sandy Richardson	Roger Tonge
Kitty Jarvis	Beryl Johnstone
Mrs Mears	Thelma Rogers
Brian Jarvis	David Fennell
Patrick Wade	Malcolm Young
Dick Jarvis	Brian Kent
George Petersham	Raymond Mason
Mrs Vi Blundell	Peggy Aitchinson

4
Emmerdale Farm –
A Breath of Fresh Air

In 1972 the government dramatically relaxed restrictions on television transmission hours, following a long campaign for more TV time. ITV immediately planned twenty extra hours of weekday TV, causing television companies to scramble for new ideas. Yorkshire TV wanted to produce a twice-weekly soap, so they asked author and playwright Kevin Laffen to write a series for them.

No one expected the result to last longer than a year or two – but that was sixteen years ago, and *Emmerdale Farm* has triumphed over such early scepticism to produce more than 1,000 entertaining episodes. The appeal is simple, really: for city dwellers, the show mirrors their own idyllic views of country life, while country folk are quite interested in television's representation of their lives.

Finding the Farm
A series set on farmland but filmed in a studio wouldn't be terribly convincing, reasoned the series' producers, so it was decided early on to film half of most programmes on location. Yorkshire TV sent an army of researchers to comb the beautiful Yorkshire dales, looking for a village and farm within short travelling distance of the Leeds studios where interiors are filmed.

These hunters turned up Arthur Bell's 200-acre farm, which matched that described in Kevin Laffen's scripts. Spacious enough for the outside broadcast vehicles, Bell's farm came replete with lambs, hens, geese

and 20 acres of barley and hay, from which Bell earns his living.

Bell was soon sorry he'd signed a thirteen-week contract with YTV! His farmyard disappeared under cables and crowds of technicians. Bell and his wife and son were besieged by cameras, vans, light rigs, cars and more than sixty people swarming across the farm. When his contract was up, Bell refused to renew it, but was persuaded by the producers to continue. After sixteen years, Bell has grown so used to the goings on that he says he hardly notices them, and has become friends with many members of the cast and crew.

The village originally chosen for outside filming was not so accommodating. After its first year, local residents bombarded YTV with complaints about coachloads of tourists and demanded the show change its location. The production crew found the beautiful village of Elshot as a replacement – the show's scripts explained the village's new look by citing structural damage to the pub. With a new pub, the Woolpack (actually the Commercial Inn), the series settled down to stay.

Down on the Farm
Our view of life at Emmerdale begins when Jacob Sugden's life ends. His wife Annie tries to keep the farm going with the aid of her family. Daughter Peggy is happily married to shepherd Matt. Sam, Annie's father, lives on the farm but can't do as much as he used

Emmerdale Farm.

to. Jack and Joe, Annie's two sons, don't see eye-to-eye and often worry Annie more than help her. Also on tap are Amos Brearly, the friendly local publican, and the local squire, Henry Wilks, who lives with his daughter Marion.

Marion and Jack have an affair. Matt and Peggy produce twins, Sally and Sam, but the farm's happiness changes to gloom as the twins die in a car crash and Peggy soon passes away without warning. Henry Wilks's house burns down and he moves in with Amos at the Woolpack. He also takes an interest in Emmerdale Farm and becomes friends with Annie.

Joe marries Christine Sharp from the Milk Board. Jack seeks the bright lights of London, then goes off to Rome to become a writer. Joe divorces Christine. Matt meets Dolly, whose illegitimate son has been adopted elsewhere, but nothing can sway him from his love and they marry. Farming giant North Yorkshire Estates sets up an office in Beckindale.

Jack returns, now a famous author, with a renewed interest in farming. Joe takes a job with NY Estates as assistant to Alan Turner, the J.R. Ewing of the Dales. Jack's former girlfriend Pat Merrick returns to the village to live in a caravan with her daughter Sandie and son Jackie. Pat also gets a job with NY Estates and Alan Turner. Divorced from Tom Merrick, Pat again takes up with Jack and the couple plan to marry. Jackie, though, dislikes Jack and is shocked to hear from his mother that Jack is his father; Pat had been pregnant when she married Tom.

Sandie gets pregnant and leaves Beckindale for Aberdeen to give birth. Matt and Dolly have their own baby, named Sam after Annie's father. Jackie romances local village girls while Joe takes a job with NY Estates in France.

Sandie returns and gets a job at the market, working with Karen Moore. Jack begins an affair with Karen and nearly destroys his marriage before reuniting with Pat. A rude local farmer named Harry Mowlam upsets Dolly. Sandie turns to Alan Turner's son Terry for romantic thrills. Alan runs over

Jackie and seriously injures him. Mowlam is found murdered and Matt is accused of the crime, but one of Mowlam's mates confesses to robbing the NY Estates wages van and killing Mowlam, thus clearing Matt.

Joe returns to Emmerdale and gets the job of area manager. Pat Sugden is killed in a car crash four months after giving Jack a son, Robert. The village sees red when the government plans to install a nuclear dump nearby. Jackie falls down a mineshaft in the bitter winter. Jack's old flame Marion returns to the village with her Italian husband, but when he leaves on business Jack sleeps with her. She returns to Italy with her husband. His losing streak continues as Jack goes to jail for yanking down a fence at the nuclear dump-site. But after their long fight the villagers win against the government and the dump is abandoned. Jackie renews his love life by sleeping with Kathy as 1987 nears its close and in 1988, they marry.

The Not-So-Great Outdoors

Unlike *Brookside*, which also does much location shooting, *Emmerdale Farm* relies heavily on outdoor scenes, in keeping with its farm setting. The mercurial English weather plays havoc with continuity, as characters waltz on-screen from snow scenes to thunder showers to clear skies and back to snow.

'We are in the hands of the weather,' said former producer Richard Handford. 'Snow is the biggest problem – because of the tight schedule, we record the farmyard scenes for six episodes in one go over two to three days, then we go to the village and record six episodes there. Uncertain winter weather means you might have Matt and Jack leaving the farm for the pub in bright sunlight and arriving at the Woolpack in knee-deep snow.'

Seasonal changes also give the production crew nightmares. Shot two months in advance, the Christmas episodes will still have October's orange leaves on the trees, while viewers can see through their own windows nothing but grey. The solution? No close-ups of the trees!

Handford nervously remembers a beautiful summer when the show was set to film scenes in a wheatfield in late August. As the time grew near, Handford noticed harvesting in many fields and grew worried. The crew were on their holidays and couldn't be recalled for earlier shooting, so a harried Handford, concerned that harvesting would throw off the show's schedule, saw no recourse but to buy the wheatfield outright to stop its owner from harvesting. He worked out a deal whereby the farmer could buy back the field, and then the weather broke with two weeks of rain, delaying harvesting and saving the show's budget.

When Fact and Fiction Collide

To its fans *Emmerdale Farm* is a winning tale of good-hearted farm people – to its detractors it's a rather slow saga devoid of the racier affairs and realistic traumas of other series. Both camps were shocked in 1986 when the series veered into hard-hitting drama. Especially unsettling was the death of Pat Sugden, and no viewer's dismay could compare with the real grief of actor Clive Hornby.

The tale began in real life, with the pregnancy of actress Helen Weir, who plays Pat Sugden. Yorkshire TV producers opted to make Pat pregnant too, a common TV ploy. Parents Clive and Helen, who had fallen in love playing husband and wife in the series (and who later married in 1985) hoped their baby would become *Emmerdale Farm*'s youngest cast member.

All was well until YTV producers balked at the name Clive and Helen had chosen for their offspring: Thomas. Unfortunately Pat Sugden's first husband was Tom Merrick, and the producers reasoned that Pat would never name Jack's baby after her ex.

Thus, the Sugden baby was to be christened Robert. Clive and Helen, however, didn't want a confused baby on their hands, so they decided to quit the show with their baby's identity intact. But with a new baby and all the attendant expenses, this proved an unreasonable decision. Clive Hornby decided to stay with the series, and the series writers widowed him by scripting a fatal car accident for Pat Sugden.

Actors often call upon real experiences for their roles, but rarely do they play anything as close to the bone as this. Clive, as Jack, was mourning the death of Jack's wife who was, in another sense, Clive's real lover. The actor felt real pain, especially as chief mourner at Pat's funeral, but managed to carry the scenes off with admirable professionalism.

Other stars have had a different kind of real/TV confusion, the kind that takes place when fans blur actors and roles. Richard Thorp's convincing portrayal of boozing philanderer Alan Turner really brings out the surly in some people. Soon after an episode where Turner ran over Jackie Merrick, Thorp found a knife stuck through the tyres of his Range Rover and a menacing note. On another occasion, a respectable woman persisted in staring at him across a Harrogate restaurant. As she left, she shouted across the room, 'You're very nasty to Joe and you know bugger-all about farming!'

Viewers look more kindly on Hugh Manning's vicar Donald Hinton, so much so that a life-size cardboard Manning informs visitors to the vicarage where *Emmerdale Farm*'s outside scenes are shot that Reverend Hinton is *not* there to hear confessions. Persistent fans continue to write to Hugh on spiritual matters, asking for comfort or guidance. Perhaps the oddest was an eighteen-page letter from a Jehovah's Witness, including a theological work for which the writer invited Hugh's comment!

Farm Folk

The cast of *Emmerdale Farm* comes from a wide range of acting backgrounds, including many other television series, soaps and more prestigious theatre work. Helen Weir (the late Pat Sugden) trained as an actress at RADA and later worked with the Royal Shakespeare Company at Stratford-upon-Avon. Once mistaken for Cilla Black by English tourists in a Spanish bar, she has quit the series to care for her and Clive Hornby's son Thomas.

Clive himself never wanted to become an actor, and indeed trained as an accountant on leaving school. He soon chucked this to join a pop group, the Dennisons, which made a few fairly successful records and embarked on a national tour. His time in the spotlight grabbed him, so Clive spent three years at

acting school, went on to children's theatre, repertory theatre, TV and a part in the film *Yanks* with Richard Gere. He came to *Emmerdale Farm* from a West End production of Agatha Christie's *Murder at the Vicarage*. He took over from Andrew Burt to play Jack Sugden, one of two *Emmerdale Farm* characters to be played by different actors (Dolly Skilbeck is the other, played first by Katherine Baker and now by Jean Rogers).

Can you see Joe Sugden fighting Daleks? Early viewers of *Dr Who* did, as actor Frazer Hines once portrayed the assistant to the Tardis-piloting doctor. Frazer, one of the series' heart-throbs, took a two-year break from the show in 1983 in hopes of saving his marriage to stage and TV star Gemma Craven. When this failed, Frazer went back to the show; the returning Joe brought with him a new maturity and now holds a top position with NY Estates.

Because he actually knew something about farming, a rarity among the cast, ex-farmboy Freddie Pyne was one of the first actors seen on *Emmerdale Farm*. His early ambition to be a teacher was abandoned when RADA accepted him. He worked in rep, spent years with the National Theatre at the Old Vic and appeared in TV's *Dixon of Dock Green* before joining *Emmerdale Farm*. Freddie relished the moment in 1986 when, after fourteen years of Matt Skilbeck's gentility, the character was accused of murdering Harry Mowlam – it gave the actor a chance to prove his mettle.

Jean Rogers, who became Dolly Skilbeck when Kathy Baker left the series, was always cast as little boys in radio plays because her voice was so light and boyish. Friday nights at the cinema gave her the acting bug at a young age. Accepted by drama school at seventeen, Jean later worked for the National Theatre, in radio on *Listen with Mother* and on *Crossroads*.

Awful Alan Turner is played by Richard Thorp, who's not rotten at all – in fact, he turned more than a few heads as Dr Rennie in the hospital soap *Emergency Ward 10*. In the 1970s, Richard played Doug Randall, a sailor boyfriend of Vera Downend in *Crossroads*.

Clive Hornby who plays Jack Sugden.

His other credits include the TV series *Family at War* and *To the Manor Born*, and films like *The Dam Busters* and *The Barretts of Wimpole Street*. Unlike Turner, Richard is married with five children, and has a customised motor bike festooned with lights.

Also in *Family at War* was Diana Davies, who now plays Alan Turner's long-suffering secretary Caroline Bates. Caroline was scheduled to appear in only twenty episodes, but the writers loved the character's snappy dialogue and kept her on. Diana has also been seen in the school programme *How We Used To Live*, and in fact is a *Coronation Street* graduate from the 1970s, when she played a shop assistant named Norma Ford with a crush on Ken Barlow. Diana was divorced in 1978, an experience which left her emotionally shattered but prepared her to play Caroline's divorce.

A tide of get-well cards flooded in for Jackie Merrick when the character was hurt in a motor-bike accident, proving the popularity of actor Ian Sharrock. Ian and Pam

Diana Davies (Caroline Bates).

Ronald Magill (Amos Brearly) and Arthur Pentelow (Henry Wilks) of the Woolpack Inn.

Grand-dad, Matt, Dolly and Annie.

Sharrock, of YTV public relations, were married at Leeds Cathedral in 1985 and the couple have a baby daughter Natalie.

Accident-prone Jackie fell down a mine-shaft in 1987 – Ian wasn't asked to duplicate this, but the shooting proved painful anyway, as sub-zero location shooting froze the actor's lips! Unable to deliver his lines, Ian was thawed with mouthfuls of hot soup.

Ronald Magill was brought up in an orphanage in Birmingham, and worked in a brass foundry and a tyre company after school. When war broke out, Ronald joined the Royal Corps of Signals, became involved in camp shows and later joined the stars in battledress. After the war he pursued acting with theatre work and roles in TV's *Special Branch* and *Perkins Patch*.

Not normally one of the series heart-throbs, it came as some surprise when Ronald discovered that his *Emmerdale Farm* character, Woolpack landlord Amos Brearly, is massively popular in Sweden! A Swedish ferry company whisked Ronald out to promote their tours, and after lengthy photo shoots Ronald found himself boogying the night away in discos, wondering 'What would Amos say?'

His early acting career was hard enough for Arthur Pentelow to need between-role jobs selling ice-cream and sliced bread, even collecting washing. His TV boom eventually came and he appeared in *Z Cars*, *Emergency Ward 10*, *Budgie* and *Coronation Street*, as well as films such as *Charlie Bubbles*, *Privilege* and *The Peace Game*. Playing proud grandfather Henry Wilks, Arthur started yearning for grandchildren of his own – not likely right now, as both his sons are in their thirties and engrossed in their work. Nick plays saxophone with Chas and Dave, while Simon is a freelance photographer.

One of the newest cast members is Malandra Burrow (Kathy Bates), who had a brief walk-on as a girlfriend of Pat Hancock in *Brookside*. She was thrown on her first day of *Emmerdale Farm* filming when she saw throngs of huge cows lurking about the farm – though she's now used to lambs and calves, Malandra is unaccountably petrified by cows, which she must occasionally pluck up the courage to milk on-screen. Not really what you'd call an animal lover, Malandra also hates hens, and perversely, Kathy once held a job in NY Estates poultry unit. Facing 20,000 hens in a shed was not Malandra's idea of a good time, and though Kathy has left the job Malandra is off eggs for life.

The Woolpack Inn.

Reaping Success

Sleepy though it may sometimes seem, *Emmerdale Farm* has moved with the times. In 1987, the public and press applauded a dramatic twist – the threat of a nuclear dump at Emmerdale, nuclear power being, until then, one of the soap taboos. The threat of a field with an afterlife has stirred the farm community into an anti-nuclear campaign.

Emmerdale Farm has also taken advantage of cable. It is shown on the British satellite channel 'Super Channel' across Europe. The series has also received a boost from new producer Stuart Doughty, who came to the series in 1987 after his successes at *Brookside*. Despite a feeling that it's in the minor league among the major soaps, the programme dealt an early blow to supersoap extraordinaire *EastEnders*. Originally, *EastEnders* was shown in the same time slot by the BBC – 7 p.m. Tuesday and Thursday. In the first weeks *Emmerdale Farm* crippled *EastEnders*' ratings so badly that the Beeb moved their fledgling series to 7.30 p.m. (It has since been moved again to 6.30 p.m. on Wednesday and Thursday.)

With a regular ten million viewers, *Emmerdale Farm* shows no signs of succumbing in the soap wars, and will continue to delight fans in the years to come.

Emmerdale Farm

First episode credits:
Transmitted 16 October, 1972
Produced by Michael Russell
Created by Kevin Laffen
A Yorkshire Television Production

Present Cast List

Character	Actor
Annie Sugden	Sheila Mercier★
Henry Wilks	Arthur Pentelow★
Matt Skilbeck	Frederick Pyne★
Amos Brearly	Ronald Magill★
Joe Sugden	Frazer Hines★
Jack Sugden	Clive Hornby
Jackie Merrick	Ian Sharrock
Sandie Merrick	Jane Hutcheson
Alan Turner	Richard Thorp
Caroline Bates	Diana Davies
Kathy Bates	Malandra Burrows
Dolly Skilbeck	Jean Rogers
Seth Armstrong	Stan Richards
Sam Skilbeck	Benjamin Whitehead

★ Original members of the cast.

Previous page *The Sugden family of* Emmerdale Farm.

Above *A picnic down on the farm.*

5
Dallas –
The Americans Invade

No one would think of comparing cuddly John-Boy Walton with slimy J.R. Ewing. But in fact, John-Boy is one of J.R.'s ancestors. Lorimar Studios' international success with *The Waltons*, a family-based one-hour drama, led the studio to accept David Jacobs's idea for a Texas family drama.

Jacobs tried first to sell the studios on a family drama based in Los Angeles, but the studios didn't like it. (They would later buy it as *Knots Landing*, the Dallas spin-off.) But the idea of a rich and powerful Texan family who lusted for power, a sort of inverted Waltons, grabbed them. Once again there would be the older generation and their voices of reason, represented by Jock and Miss Ellie Ewing, presiding over their more interesting children, Bobby and J.R.

But there the similarities with other TV families would end. Gone were the homespun homilies of both *The Waltons* and prototypical American TV families from *Father Knows Best* to *Leave it to Beaver*. Paul Henning, creator of another rich backwoods clan, The Clampetts from *The Beverly Hillbillies*, once said people will only tune in week after week to see people they like. *Dallas* would aim to bring people back week after week to see someone they hated.

Lorimar wasn't gambling that much: J.R. wasn't as pre-eminent in the early scripts and the series wasn't a soap opera, just a mini-series. A rash of these, such as *Rich Man, Poor Man*, had proved the popularity of fat, exotic dramas of power.

Larry Hagman who plays J.R. Ewing and Linda Gray who plays his wife Sue Ellen.

Once he received Lorimar's go-ahead, producer Leonard Katzman began scouting Texas for Southfork Ranch, a domicile worthy of the expansive Ewings. In winter 1977 he arrived in Dallas to find it under four feet of snow from one its worst winters, which cramped his quest. He found, in fact,

49

two Southfork Ranches – one for exterior shots (Box Ranch) and one for interior filming ('Swish House' on Swish Avenue).

Star Search

With that settled, Katzman returned for the casting. One role seemed to be taken care of – before it was called *Dallas* (or even *Houston* – the working title changed for greater impact) the programme was known as 'The Linda Evans Project'. Linda was under contract to CBS, and was presumed to get the then-central role of Pam Ewing. *Dallas* was, in fact, created as a Linda Evans vehicle, but as the project progressed and Pam's role dwindled to something 'unworthy' of Linda's talent (or salary), the idea of using her was dropped. Come *Dynasty*, of course, she wouldn't care at all.

The senior roles went to Barbara Bel Geddes, a Hollywood film veteran and a much bigger name in the theatre at the time, and Jim Davis, star of several B-movies. Steve Kanaly was originally considered for Bobby, but the producers scored by landing Patrick Duffy, fresh out of the water from his stint on *The Man From Atlantis*. Steve Kanaly ended up as Ray and Ken Kercheval became Cliff Barnes.

Unknown Linda Gray beat out the better-known Mary Franny for the Sue Ellen role; the part wouldn't really get going until Linda started warming up her notorious 'Sue Ellen looks'. Five-foot-tall Charlene Tilton was cast as Lucy, but her size became a problem. It meant she had to play many scenes standing on an apple crate.

How different might the world have been had Robert Foxworth been chosen as J.R. The handsome star of *The Black Marble*, *Prophecy* and other films almost took the part, but felt the role should be softened. This didn't fit in with the *Dallas* plan (fortunately!), so the producers went with Larry Hagman, the long-suffering straight man of the 1960s comedy series, *I Dream of Jeannie*. Being known primarily for a comic part could have hindered Larry's success in a sinister role; it's to his credit as an actor that he convinced the world he was really a nasty, nasty person.

Because of *The Man From Atlantis*, not an incredibly popular series but a recent one, Patrick Duffy was thought to be the real star attraction in the *Dallas* cast. A story that appeared in the *Dallas Morning News* when the show began filming didn't even mention Larry Hagman.

Dallas Fever

The mini-series premiered on 2 April 1978 and ran for five Sunday nights, receiving impressive ratings for an unknown show. CBS immediately signed a deal with Lorimar to make *Dallas* a regular series with soap-style continuity, beginning in September 1978. This decision might have backfired – mini-series were at the time a hotter property than most regular series – but instead launched a programme of immense influence, popular the world over, avidly watched by foreign citizens who didn't even know where Dallas was.

One sign of success was *Dallas*'s almost immediate import to the UK. The BBC bought the mini-series and the first season, and began transmitting the whole saga on 5 September 1978. The series rapidly became the hottest American drama in the British Isles; thanks to Radio Two DJ Terry Wogan, who treated his daily listeners to the goings-on at Southfork.

Behind the Scenes

With *Dallas* an assured success and a major part of the CBS 1978/9 line-up, the cast and crew embark on one of television's most gruelling schedules. Filming starts in June/July, with interior shots done in Los Angeles studios and exteriors in Texas. In order to save time in *Dallas*, whole blocks of exteriors for many episodes are shot back-to-back on six-day work-weeks.

Los Angeles is no picnic in the summer, but Texas is unbearable. Temperatures may soar above 100°F. Actors fall prey to sun stroke, gulp salt tablets to keep from sweating in front of the cameras, and are ferried in and out of air-conditioned trailers. While the crew sport shorts and sleeveless shirts, stars must waltz about in leather, three-piece suits and other uncomfortable clothes dreamed up by wardrobe.

Production for the series now runs fifty-one weeks; the writers get Christmas week off, and that's all. Strict security surrounds

Dallas scripts, as the press will try any means to leak the series' surprises. Pages with absolutely top-secret happenings are handed out on a need-to-know basis only and stamped 'For Your Eyes Only'. At the beginning of each season there is a 'Bible' filled with notes on each character and where he or she is going. Copies distributed to top Lorimar executives are kept under lock and key.

One *Dallas* episode takes seven preparation days and seven shoot days – directors alternate episodes for maximum overlap and efficiency. Make-up call is at 5.30 a.m., with the first shot at 8 a.m. and the day's close at 6.30 p.m. Retakes are permitted but schedule over-runs are not – unless real disaster strikes, the director must shoot all the shots detailed for that day, as *Dallas*'s precarious schedule depends on it. For their pains *Dallas* directors are paid approximately $15,000 for two weeks' work.

As much as eight weeks can pass between filming of scenes that will appear next to each other in an episode, due to the separate filming of exterior and interior shots and the block method of shooting scenes. These time lags put a strain on such continuity-conscious people as the make-up staff. 'We try to make every one up as perfect as possible,' says make-up man Joe Haily, but matching shades on scenes shot wildly out of sequence taxes their organisational skills.

The actresses don't use traditional film make-up, but use over-the-counter brands. One of the trickier tasks for Haily and his staff is the 'no make-up look', used for the soused Sue Ellen or the jailed Jenna (Priscilla Presley), for example. Women realise that the no make-up look takes even longer to achieve than the regular make-up look. In all, *Dallas*'s make-up bill generally reaches $5,000 to $7,500 a year.

Clothes are covered in another chapter – suffice it to say here that *Dallas* sports an extremely expensive and fashionable wardrobe. Make that two wardrobes: in case an article of clothing is damaged, the wardrobe department buys two of everything.

The Real Southfork Ranch

Though not many realise it, the Ewings moved in 1979. *Dallas* had only run for a year when Katzman and Lorimar were faced with the challenge of finding a new Southfork Ranch. Filming had moved to Duncan Acres in Plano, Texas, when *Dallas* became a regular series, and after one season the owners of Box Ranch complained that the camera crews were making business impossible and they wanted out. Katzman, scouring Dallas from a helicopter, spotted a 200-acre ranch just north of the city. He landed in the front garden (everything *is* bigger in Texas, you know) and began negotiations with the owner John Duncan.

As they say in those parts, there are no flies on John Duncan. The real-estate tycoon built the ranch in 1970 as his home and working ranch, and saw how affiliation with the *Dallas* programme might work in his favour. Not long after his ranch became known as Southfork to millions of viewers, Duncan turned it into a Texas tourist attraction, the home of the Ewings.

Run by assistant manager Hugh Elmore, the ranch is visited by some 2,000 people a day. These paying guests soak up the oil-rich atmosphere and can stand on such historic spots as the balcony from which J.R. pushed Kristin into the pool. Those with cash to burn can spend the night at Southfork and breakfast in Ewing style for around $2,500. Sue Ellen's services are not included.

Love, Oil and Money

The *Dallas* saga begins in 1978, when Bobby Ewing, son of Jock and Ellie Ewing, brings home Pamela Jean Barnes to Southfork Ranch. Bobby and Pam had wed in New Orleans, after meeting at the Ewing barbecue, where Pam had been Ray Krebbs's date. Bobby had been Ewing Oil's road man while his brother J.R. ran the firm, having taken over after Jock's retirement.

A frosty reception welcomes Bobby and Pam to Southfork Ranch. Pam is, after all, a Barnes, and the Ewings have feuded with the Barnes since 1860. Bobby joins the family oil firm at home, much against power-hungry J.R.'s wishes. J.R. is married to a former Miss Texas, Sue Ellen. Also at Southfork is Lucy Ewing, daughter of the middle Ewing son Gary, black sheep of the clan, and his wife Val.

Digger and Cliff Barnes, Pam's father and brother, do their best to blacken the Ewing name, believing the Ewings have cheated them out of an oil fortune. Plus, Cliff and arch-enemy J.R. (who usually gets the upper hand in their wranglings) have a nasty habit of sharing women: first Julie Gray, who is found murdered, then Sue Ellen. When she becomes pregnant, Cliff is suspected to be the father, to J.R.'s horror. He has her taken to a sanatarium, but Sue Ellen is not to be underestimated. Her next affair, with cowboy Dusty Farlow, ends when Dusty seems to die in a plane crash, but he returns later for more Sue Ellen. J.R. and Sue Ellen finally divorce. Gary and Valene Ewing remarry and move away.

The late 1970s are a busy time for the Ewings. Jock has a heart attack, Ellie has a mastectomy, and Pam finds out Digger is not her father – Digger has murdered her real father, Hutch McKinney, and unsuccessfully blamed Jock. While she takes off to find her mother (Rebecca Wentworth), Bobby becomes a Texan Senator. Sue Ellen bears John Ross while J.R. dallies with Holly Harwood, Mandy Winger and Afton Cooper.

Complications in the family lives continue when Ray is found to be Jock's son and marries Donna Culver, while Lucy marries Afton's brother Mitch. Meanwhile, J.R. is shot, and after a suspenseful summer the world learns Kristin Shepard, Sue Ellen's sister, did it, because J.R. dumped her after their affair.

Wheelchair-bound, J.R. temporarily surrenders Ewing Oil to Bobby, but not for long. Jock goes off into the jungle to find oil. J.R. exacts revenge by pushing Kristin into the Ewing pool. Cliff Barnes tries to save her but she's dead. Cliff's mother gives him a company and Cliff embezzles to fund a revenge scheme on J.R., at which point his mother takes the company back! She later buys him an oil company of his own.

Pam and Bobby adopt Kristin's child Christopher – J.R. is the suspected dad. Rebecca Wentworth dies in a plane crash, and Jock perishes in a jungle accident. Jock's will sets up a deadly rivalry between J.R. and Bobby, a winner-take-all duel for the company.

Sue Ellen and J.R. divorce, with her keeping John Ross; they later remarry, but his infidelity causes her to crash her car. Cliff

Barnes attempts suicide. His and Pam's half-sister, Katherine Wentworth, falls in love with Bobby, who is himself smitten with his old flame, Jenna Wade. Sue Ellen sleeps with Cliff. Miss Ellie gets married again, to Dusty's father Clayton, despite interference by J.R. and Lady Jessica Montford, Clayton's mad sister.

Pam, getting a bit more like Sue Ellen every year, meets and falls in love with Mark Graison. The dying man, however, is lost and possibly dead after his plane crashes. Things heat up when jealous Katherine shoots Bobby, temporarily blinding him. Afton finds him and has him taken to the hospital, where Katherine tries to give him a lethal injection. J.R. stops her and Katherine goes missing while Bobby gets his sight back. Pam, convinced by J.R. that Mark is alive, takes off on a wild goose chase to find him, but fails.

Jenna is accused of murdering her former husband Renaldo Marchetta, but Bobby proves she was framed. Cliff attempts to take over Ewing Oil, but fails. After Lucy and Mitch marry, for the second time, Pam and Bobby get back together. Bobby seems to be slain by Katherine Wentworth, but this and succeeding events (one year's-worth for the series) turn out to be merely Pam's dream. She awakes to find Bobby in her shower.

Sue Ellen goes into the underwear business, but must still compete for J.R.'s affections against a host of rivals, including Mandy Winger. Pam remarries Bobby and learns that, at last, she can bear children of her own. She phones Bobby, breaks the good news, and collides with an oil tanker. The *Dallas* epic continues without her. The 1987/8 season features renewed battling between J.R. and Cliff, who is again romancing Sue Ellen and trying to gain custody of John Ross.

Who Shot J.R.?

Dallas was, by 1980, the most popular television series in the world. Small towns in Wales sold J.R. dartboards. Restaurants and cafes in Italy were deserted on *Dallas* nights. The members of Turkey's parliament cut short a meeting so they could rush home and catch an episode. The Bonn Municipal

Theatre in West Germany wrote and produced a forty-five minute ballet based on the Ewing exploits. Was there anywhere to go from this pinnacle of TV-mania?

Yes. Lorimar and Katzman hadn't planned to shoot the moon, but when CBS demanded an additional two episodes of the series beyond what was planned for 1980, Katzman and Executive Producer Philip Caprice (creator David Jacobs had left) scrapped the original suspenseful season close and came up with the surprise cliff-hanger known the world over as 'Who Shot J.R.?'

For one feverish summer, that was *the* question as mystery-buffs everywhere looked for clues. Not many were presented in the actual programme, where J.R. is working late at the office, hears a sound and is fired upon by an unseen assailant. Most of the cast had a reason for wanting to shoot J.R., with prime suspects being Sue Ellen, her sister Kristin, Cliff Barnes, the members of the oil cartel and even Bobby.

The result was television history, as 83 million people watched the shooting in the US and 24 million in the UK. When the answer was broadcast in the autumn, 83 million Americans again tuned in . . . but 27.3 million watched in Britain. Somehow, during those three months, 3.3 million of us who hadn't seen J.R. get shot found we *needed* to know who did it! Many viewers perhaps wanted to see if J.R. would die, but anyone who can draw those kind of ratings isn't going anywhere. Realising this, Larry Hagman renegotiated his contract for a pay rise – no fool he. Reports stated his new salary as $1 million per year.

The producers had considered replacing Larry, possibly with Robert Culp (of *I Spy*) but Hagman proved too good to let go. Few *Dallas* actors are deemed irreplaceable, though, as proven by the number of characters who have been portrayed by multiple actors. Barbara Bel Geddes and Donna Reed both played Ellie Ewing, a major role, while Gary Ewing has looked like both Ted Shackleford and David Ackroyd. Keenan Wynn and David Wayne were successively Digger Barnes; Mary Crosby and Colleen Camp had their shots at Kristin Shepard, Susan French and Lesley Woods took on Amanda

Larry Hagman with his off-screen Swedish wife Maj at London airport.

Ewing, while Jenna Wade has been characterised by three actresses: Morgan Fairchild, Francine Tacker and Priscilla Presley.

Just a Bunch of Good Old Boys and Gals

More than any other star of *Dallas*, Larry Hagman has been catapulted to fame by his role. A recognised comic actor due to his role as Major Anthony Nelson in *I Dream of Jeannie*, he has also had a number of straight film roles, including his finest as a government translator in Sidney Lumet's spellbinding anti-nuke caveat *Failsafe*.

Larry's mother is famed stage actress Mary Martin, of *South Pacific* fame – Larry hoped she could play Miss Ellie when Barbara Bel Geddes gave up the role, but it was not to be. A married man for thirty-four years, Larry proposed to his Swedish wife Maj in 1954 on his birthday. They met when Larry was in the American Air Force in London, and now have two children.

He's taken his share of scorn for his villainous role, but the real 'J.R.' is nothing like his character. Known as 'Wacky Larry' or 'Lawrence of Malibu', he delights in antics such as parading near his Southern California home dressed as a British copper, a Chinese coolie and a French foreign legionnaire. He got used to bizarre costumes during his slapstick years as the beleaguered Major Nelson.

Larry has nothing but respect for his *Dallas* role; he may slight J.R.'s business sense ('J.R. has lost Ewing Oil more than 16 million dollars,' says Larry), but he can't put down J.R.'s taste in women. Besides Sue Ellen, J.R. has dallied with Kristin Shepard (Mary Crosby), Sally Bullock (Joanna Cassidy), Louella Howard (Meg Gallagher), Afton Cooper (Audrey Landers), Marilee Stone (Fern Fitzgerald), Katherine Wentworth (Morgan Brittany), Holly Harwood (Lois Chiles), Mandy Winger (Deborah Shelton), Angelica Nero (Barbara Carrera) and his latest flame, Kimberley Cryder (Leigh Taylor Young). No wonder business suffers!

Winner of second place for All-Time Resurrection Achievement surely must go to Patrick Duffy. First he asked to be killed, then once dead, he asked to come back, and did! Patrick was sick of Bobby Ewing after seven years, and longed to pursue his neglected film career. This fizzled: he made a series of commercials for British TV rental firm DER, a British mini-series called *Strong Medicine* and a flop film, *Vamping*. But his real-estate projects kept him in the black.

Things weren't going so well at *Dallas*. Despite an impressive death scene and funeral, ratings dropped with Bobby dead.

Victoria Principal (Pamela Ewing) who played Bobby Ewing's wife in the series.

Larry Hagman sought out Patrick and persuaded him to return. Patrick returned the favour with practical jokes on his friend Larry. He had the film crew spread the rumour that the ranch was infested with rattlesnakes, then slipped a rubber one into Larry's boot. The screams when J.R. donned his boots on-screen brought filming to a standstill.

Patrick has been married for fifteen years to his wife, Carlyn, and they have two children. The *Dallas* actor's salary is alleged to reach $75,000 a season. Sadly, his happy return to the series was shattered when his parents were shot dead at their Boulder bar in November 1986. Terry and Marie Duffy, both in their sixties, were murdered when they confronted two drunk teenage hooligans. The killers were later captured by the police.

Bobby came back – can Pam? That's what viewers have been wondering since Pam Ewing's demise in the 1986/7 season. Unwilling to be fooled again, audiences suspended their belief when Pam, after telling Bobby on her car phone that she can now have children, drove into a tanker lorry.

If she does return, rumour has it Pam will be played by a new actress. Certainly there is no reason for Victoria Principal to return: the series has made the actress a celebrity, her name and face attached as much to talk shows, exercise spas and beauty books as to her television role. Litigation has also kept her name in the news – Victoria sued Joan Rivers for giving out her telephone number on national television, after Joan accused Victoria of lying about her age.

Victoria, despite her association with health and working-out, was forced to take time off the series a few seasons ago when an old back problem flared up. She married Dr Harry Glassman in 1985 – his expertise is not back troubles but plastic surgery, something Victoria certainly doesn't need. Victoria recently made quite a splash as the title character in the serious television film *Mistress*.

Linda Gray has steadily built up her role as Sue Ellen, which was little more than decorative when the show began. She has also directed an episode, and a tough one at that, featuring a masquerade ball and two deaths besides the usual romance and revenge. Not

Ken Kercheval (Cliff Barnes) and his wife Ava Fox at the start of their European honeymoon.

bad for a woman who started acting in her thirties.

In real life, Linda is good friends with screen husband Larry Hagman, and the two have appeared together on Terry Wogan's show. She has two children whom she raises alone, after the break up of her marriage with Ed Thrasher. Some have suggested her sultry beauty and on-screen slow burns would suit rival series *Dynasty*, but Linda insists Sue Ellen wouldn't be happy there: 'There would never be enough booze or clean glasses to keep her going.'

At sixteen Barbara Bel Geddes was expelled from high school for being 'a disturbing influence'. This is our Miss Ellie? Told she wasn't sexy enough for Hollywood, she stuck it out on the stage there until forced to nurse her second husband, who died from cancer. After his death Barbara won the role of the female head of the Ewing family. When Jim Davis (Jock Ewing) died of a brain tumour, it was as if she had lost another husband.

Barbara herself has suffered from ill health. She has had a lump on her breast removed, then relived the experience as screenwriters forced Miss Ellie to have the same thing. Following a heart attack, Barbara had a quadruple-bypass heart operation, forcing her to take a break from the series and give up smoking (she could formerly go through as many as seventy cigarettes a day).

In her place came Donna Reed, but unlike Larry Hagman, Donna's goody-goody image was set in concrete from years of 1950s sitcoms. Viewers didn't buy the replacement and Donna lasted but one season. When Barbara agreed to come back, Donna was made redundant. She sued CBS Entertainment and Lorimar Productions for breach of contract to the tune of $7.5 million, but tragically died of cancer soon thereafter. When Barbara returned to the series, determined to lead a fitter life, viewers and actors rejoiced.

Health problems of a different sort plagued Ken Kercheval prior to his days as Cliff Barnes. An alcoholic for years, he checked into a detoxification centre a year before he began *Dallas*, and later shocked his co-stars by revealing on a national talk show that he was a member of Alcoholics Anonymous, and by stating that drinking was a killing disease.

Ken's career had several false starts: he sold encyclopaedias, photographed babies, sold cemetery plots and helped build a sewer tunnel under New York City before finding acting fame. With his drinking problem licked, Ken has time to concentrate on his loves in life: his wife Ava Fox, car repair and his own popcorn farm.

Recent press reports had Ken calling Cliff Barnes a wimp and threatening to walk off the series if his character didn't improve. Allegedly appalled at the way Cliff was constantly outwitted, even by new characters such as Dandy Dandridge, Ken demanded a return to form for Cliff. The producers seem to have taken his suggestions to heart, as the 1987/8 season rekindled the Cliff/Sue Ellen romance and featured a tougher, stronger Cliff going after custody of John Ross.

Ken Kercheval was, in fact, originally cast as Ray Krebbs, with Steve Kanaly cast as Bobby Ewing, but when Patrick Duffy came into the picture Ken and Steve were shuffled. Steve made quite an impression in the first mini-series, rolling around with Lucy Ewing.

He rather lucked into acting, after a debilitating experience in Vietnam. Days without food or water were commonplace. When his bunker was hit by an enemy rocket, the three men with him died and Steve was left with a compressed vertebra, preventing him from playing some sports. Being a crack army shot, he returned to the States to become a clay-pigeon-shooting instructor. At the shooting range he met film director John Milius, who used some of Steve's war experiences when writing *Apocalypse Now*. Through Milius Steve met the late John

Huston, who cast him in *Judge Roy Bean*. After several film roles, Steve was cast as the hard-working Ewing rancher. He and wife Brent have two children.

Susan Howard was shocked when told at the end of the 1986/7 season that her character, Donna Culver Krebbs, was 'surplus to requirements' after seven years, and being written out. One problem may have been with Susan, not Donna – she feels the producers resented her overt love of religion. She and her second husband, film executive Calvin Crane, pray together and say that God helps them deal with their problems. Susan's devotion kept her character on the straight and narrow: unlike her on-screen compatriots, Donna Krebbs steered clear of stray beds and bottles.

Lucy Ewing left *Dallas* simultaneously with Bobby, but in far less dramatic fashion – she simply married and moved away. Still, it came as a shock to Charlene Tilton, who has enjoyed her role on *Dallas* since her start

Charlene Tilton who played Lucy Ewing.

as a teenager. She was hoping to wangle a part on *Knots Landing*, but didn't. Instead she took a part in a play in San Francisco.

The youngest member of the cast at one time, Charlene made tabloid news several times. She lost vast sums of money due to poor financial management, and one of her accountants was jailed for embezzlement. Her marriage to country singer Johnny Lee exploded in court when Charlene accused Lee of battering her and Lee called her a religious fanatic. Charlene's 'party girl' image has died down, and she is now married to singer Dominic Allen, nephew of Scottish entertainer Jimmy Logan. The couple have a daughter, Cherish.

The most recent gossip was that Charlene would return to *Dallas*. This rumour seems

Morgan Brittany (Katherine Wentworth) and her real-life husband Jack Gill.

Sheree Wilson played Jack Ewing's ex-wife.

to have come from none other than Ms Tilton – it even took Leonard Katzman by surprise! Lucy fans will be pleased to hear that she is returning to the series.

Many soap stars are stunned by the tremendous fame and wealth their roles bring. Not so Priscilla Presley – compared to what she knew with her ex-husband Elvis, *Dallas* has made her an unknown! As a Presley, she has seen how the awestruck and the greedy can betray the famous, and is moved by the ability to make good friends with the stars of *Dallas*. Her new success has also helped her cope with being in the public eye.

As the wife (from age fourteen) and then widow of one of this century's biggest celebrities, Priscilla has lived through a firestorm of often hurtful publicity. Her own book on her life with Elvis shocked even her parents with her revelations regarding their sexual experimentation. Priscilla inherited $9 million from the late rock 'n' roller, while their daughter Lisa Marie received $35 million and Elvis's estate. Priscilla also has a son, Navarone, by her live-in lover Marco Gribaldi.

When Jim Davis died, the show faced a major gap, one the producers thankfully chose not to fill with a new Jock. Instead they installed Howard Keel as Clayton Farlow, father of Sue Ellen's lover Lusty Dusty and soon Miss Ellie's husband. Howard, now in his seventies, starred in the stage version of *Oklahoma* and in such Hollywood attractions as *Seven Brides for Seven Brothers*. His third marriage has lasted some eighteen years and he and wife Judy have a teenaged daughter, Lesley.

Omri Katz, the young star who plays John Ross, has a 'foster father' in Larry Hagman, who plays his screen father. When Omri's real father was imprisoned on a cocaine charge, Larry took Omri under his wing, helped him with his school work and even taught him to swim at the *Dallas* ranch's pool. Omri's father calls Larry 'the guardian angel', and thanked Larry and Linda Gray via satellite when the pair were on Wogan's show in Christmas 1986. One more J.R. myth down the drain.

But the fans who think J.R.'s a slippery weasel will be vindicated by this story involving the man and his girlfriend Mandy Winger, played by former Miss USA Deborah Shelton. The two were making out in a bubble bath scene when the bath oil and slick tub made them slip and slide out of control when they tried to kiss. The crew had to anchor the frustrated actors with sandbags to film the shot.

Many actresses might have been mortified but not Deborah. She's not the wilting willow her beauty queen title might suggest – in fact, she's a former tobacco-chewing tomboy who played American football at her home in Norfolk, Virginia. She married Israeli record-producer Shaki Levy in 1977 after a twenty-three-day whirlwind romance, and ended her break from *Dallas* when tons of fanmail demanded her return.

Katherine Wentworth is a dedicated hunter – having failed to kill Bobby in real life, she even went after him in Pam's dreams! Morgan Brittany herself began her acting career at age five in commercials, and had walk-on parts in Hitchcock's *The Birds* and the forgettable *Yours, Mine and Ours* with

Dack Rambo who plays Jack Ewing.

Henry Fonda. In later years her career dried up, and a despondent twenty-two-year-old Morgan headed for New York where she began making commercials again. Good fortune found her being cast for *Dallas*. Morgan is married to stuntman Jack Gill and the couple have a daughter, Katherine Elizabeth.

The naughtier her role gets, the more Shreei Wilson enjoys it – which is why she has such a ball on *Dallas*, playing April Stevens, Jack Ewing's ex-wife. The former high school cheerleader and gymnast was first seen on TV commercials, and then in a small role as a therapist in *Tootsie* with Dustin Hoffman, set around a long-running soap opera. To preserve her youthful beauty, Shreei works out every day with weights and aerobics.

Now that Patrick Duffy is back, Jack Ewing has taken a bit of a backseat in the cast again, which doesn't please Dack Rambo – he once campaigned to have his name in the opening credits. Dack is haunted by the death of his twin brother Dirk in 1972, the

victim of a drunk driver. The resultant shock sent Dack to a therapist in an attempt to deal with his grief.

Charlene McCall calls Charlie Wade 'the stupidest kid ever! All she ever says is 'Hi! John Ross! Hi, Bobby, Where's J.R.?' Another ex-beauty pageant winner, Charlene accepts such banalities to play opposite her TV mother, Priscilla Presley, whom she loves, and for a shot at the glory that accompanies being a *Dallas* star.

Dream a Little Dream of Me

Dallas's fantastic popularity extends even to anti-American areas. In 1985, American hostages in Beirut were amazed to see their terrorist captors huddled around the television set for that country's first season of *Dallas*. The terrorists seemed to like J.R. best, which makes sense.

Its story-lines, however weak, are therefore transmitted to millions around the globe, who are as familiar with the series' plot convulsions of 1985/6 as with their own nation's politics.

Patrick Duffy, tired of the series after nearly ten years, quit. Filmically, this translated into the tragic murder of Bobby Ewing.

After ditching his old flame Jenna in favour of Pam, Bobby must convince Pam that Jenna won't be a problem. When the couple spent the night together at Pam's home, however, not Jenna but Katherine Wentworth was watching. Pam's half-sister had tried to kill Bobby before, first with a gun and then with a fatal syringe. As Bobby and Pam kissed goodbye in the morning, Katherine's car sped up the driveway. Bobby heroically shoved Pam aside, taking the death blow himself. The accident took Katherine's life, and a few hours later ended Bobby's as well. Near the end, he told Pam, 'All that time wasted – we should have been married.' If your tear ducts were still dry after that, they probably flooded after Bobby's final words to the gathered Ewings: 'Be a family.'

(l to r) Joshua Harris (Christopher Ewing: Pam and Bobby's adopted son), Charlene McCall (Charlie Wade: Jenna Wade's daughter) and Omri Katz (John Ross: J.R.'s son).

After her mourning, Pam married Mark Graison, then found Bobby in her shower on the morning of her honeymoon. It was as if she were having a terrible nightmare . . .

Meanwhile, Larry Hagman had talked Patrick Duffy back into the series. Patrick, not being dead himself, could hardly have been expected to portray a dead man. But no one expected the writers and producers would go as far as they did to restore Patrick Duffy to the small screen.

The shocking twist was in fact circulated as a rumour for months before it was televised, but even those who had heard it dismissed it as too far-fetched. Nonetheless, come the autumn of 1986, the most famous shower scene since *Psycho* transpired when Pam looked in the bathroom to find Bobby asking for a towel.

Readjustment was the order of the day as a startled audience faced the prospect of the entire 1985/6 season being a dream. Critics howled with derision, non-*Dallas* fans struggled to swallow the confusing versions from shell-shocked supporters, and *Dallas* history was rewritten in the blink of an eye. Many who swallowed the sentimental death scenes hook, line and sinker felt betrayed by this ruthless resuscitation.

However, the show has never been particularly realistic, and Bobby's comeback brought the series more notoriety than it had achieved since J.R. was shot. Nor were the producers doing an unheard-of thing with the 'Pam's dream' twist: it's a favourite device of bizarre science fiction movies. As early as the 1950s the lead character of *Invaders from Mars* awakened at the film's end to find he's dreamed the entire story.

That's not to imply *Dallas*' producers weren't worried about the public's response. When they asked Larry Hagman what he thought about the dream idea, he said, 'Well, we'll either be off the air right away or the viewers will accept it.'

In 1985 British viewers were understandably puzzled and angered by a much-publicised dispute for future rights in *Dallas*. ITV's Thames Television made a bid to wrest the series from the BBC and viewers protested when several episodes were cancelled. After protracted negotiations the BBC reclaimed the series.

Ted Shackleford (Gary Ewing) with Charlene Tilton (his daughter Lucy in Dallas).

Dallas – the Sequels

Pinned above every Hollywood producer's desk must be the saying, 'Nothing Succeeds Like Success'. In TV terms, this translates into the 'one more time' philosophy of sequels and spin-offs. It wasn't long – only one year, in fact – before Lorimar and David Jacobs created a sequel to their phenomenal hit soap.

Knots Landing, the *Dallas* spin-off, was picked up by the BBC soon after its 1979 debut in the States. However, it didn't fare as well on this side of the Atlantic. Maybe we're just not as *Dallas*-hungry as the Yanks. In any event, the BBC soon ceased transmission and left it on the shelf for four years before showing KL again. It started its second UK run in 1986 as a daytime programme.

Much of the Landing's action revolves around Gary and Valene Ewing, their neighbours Karen and Sid Fairgate, Kenny and Ginger Ward, and Richard and Laura Avery. With the emphasis on love rather than power, these and other characters scheme, cheat and have passionate flings, spoiled largely by Abby Cunningham, the sneaky seductress who pursues Gary and is later matched in deviousness by Ruth Galveston. Hot story-lines included the death of Ciji Dunne, Senator Gregory Sumner's resignation to pursue Empire Valley, the Machiavellian machinations of syndicate boss Mark St Claire and the kidnapping of Val's babies (which she thought were stillborn).

Ladies and Gentlemen of the Landing

The lesser Ewings are tormented by KL's answer to *Dynasty*'s Alexis, beautiful but bitchy Abby, played by Donna Mills. Donna, the owner of a sixteen-bedroom mansion in the Hollywood Hills, has had to seek police protection against her legions of fans. In one nightmarish incident, she was harassed by threatening letters from convict Daniel Vega, who later escaped from prison but was tracked down before he could harm Donna. She has also done battle with a deadly blood-sugar condition that can cause severe depression and death, and forces her to adhere to a special diet. Bill Travilla, the

Donna Mills and William Davane who starred in Knots Landing.

dress designer for *Dallas* and KL, says Donna is the only woman he has designed for who stops traffic.

Donna apparently has much more fun in her role than former pro-basketball player and sports announcer Ted Shackleford. Ted, who took over as black-sheep brother Gary Ewing when David Ackroyd opted out of *Knots Landing*, says, 'I'm sick of Ewing's alcoholism and pathetic weaknesses. My *Knots Landing* role is boring.' He also feels the love scenes are too tame, and would like to liven them up with some nudity, preferably Donna's. Nice try, Ted.

A two-week stint on *Dallas* turned into a year's performance for Joan Van Ark, who plays goody-goody writer Valene Ewing, and then into a seven year stretch on KL. Intimidated at first by Donna Mills, Joan has become good friends with the superstar, and says, 'She's the only woman on a parallel with Joan Collins.'

Joan's five-to-ten mile runs each day have been brought into KL scripts as part of Valene's character. Joan is also very superstitious – she never walks under ladders and if someone whistles in her dressing room she goes outside, turns around three times and knocks. She and husband John Marshall live with their daughter Vanessa.

Beautiful star Michele Lee has gone through a divorce that would have made faithful-but-dizzy Karen's hair curl. After seventeen years of marriage she divorced former *Dynasty* star James Farentino, demanding $8,000 per month for her and her teenaged son. The annual expenses cited in court could have come from a *Dynasty* character: thousands of dollars each for medical/psychiatric treatment, hair, cosmetics and clothes, promotion and entertainment. Lee is now married to CBS TV network vice-president Fred Rappapot. For her remarkable performance when Sid Fairgate died, Lee used her pain at the death of her marriage.

When singer Lisa Hartman's character, singer Ciji, was killed, her murder was the cliffhanger of the season; most of the cast were suspects! With Gary Ewing her mentor, Ciji got a job in Richard Avery's restaurant, and then a recording contract. Gary loved her but she was dating Chip Roberts, Val Ewing's agent, and carrying his child. On the night of her album launch she is found dead, and a drunken Gary can't remember what he was doing.

In fact, Chip Roberts had slain her, for refusing to have an abortion. Ciji, also once accused of having a lesbian affair with Laura Avery, would not return, and 'Who Killed Ciji?' T-shirts never caught on, but Lisa Hartman was brought back by popular demand. No dreamy shower scenes, though – Lisa just took on another character, Cathy Ceary.

Pity poor Laura Avery. Probably the unluckiest lass on the Landing, she has been held at gunpoint by her husband Richard, raped, bedded by someone else's husband at his insistence, held hostage at a party and involved with Ciji. As if all this weren't enough, actress Constance McCashin found herself pregnant in the middle of one season. Her baby, Daniel, appeared in the series as Laura's baby, also named Daniel. Unlike Constance, though, Laura gave birth to her Daniel in the back of a Mercedes.

Actor James Farentino and his wife Knots Landing *star Michelle Lee, who played Karen Fairgate.*

Previous page *Barbara Bel Geddes who plays Miss Ellie Ewing in* Dallas.

Top left *Larry Hagman (J.R. Ewing) and Linda Gray (Sue Ellen).*

Top right *Patrick Duffy (Bobby Ewing) and Victoria Principal (Pamela Ewing).*

Bottom left *Steve Kanaly (Ray Krebbs) and Susan Howard (Donna Krebbs).*

Lisa Hartman who played Ciji and Cathy Ceary.

Dallas

First episode credits:
Transmitted 2 April, 1978 in US,
   5 September, 1978 in UK
Produced by Leonard Katzman
Created by David Jacobs
A Lorimar Tele Pictures Production

Original Cast List

Character	Actor
J.R. Ewing	Larry Hagman
Miss Ellie Ewing	Barbara Bel Geddes
Jock Ewing	Jim Davis
Bobby Ewing	Patrick Duffy
Pam Ewing	Victoria Principal
Sue Ellen Ewing	Linda Gray
Lucy Ewing	Charlene Tilton
Ray Krebbs	Steve Kanaly
Cliff Barnes	Ken Kercheval

Knots Landing

First episode credits:
Transmitted 27 December, 1979 in US,
   26 April, 1980 in UK
Produced by Joseph Wallenstein
Created by David Jacobs
Roundelay Productions in association
   with Lorimar Productions

Original Cast List

Character	Actor
Valene Ewing	Joan Van Ark
Gary Ewing	Ted Shackleford
Karen Fairgate	Michele Lee
Sid Fairgate	Don Murray
Laura Avery	Constance McCashin
Richard Avery	John Pleshette
Kenny Ward	James Houghton
Ginger Ward	Kim Lankford

Still More from the Lone Star State

If *Dallas* and *Knots Landing* didn't quench your desire for Ewings, more could be had with the three-hour prequel, *Dallas: The Early Years*. Telecast in 1984 by Lorimar, this $2 million epic was first released on video in the UK, and later shown on TV. It was strictly an extra snack for diehard *Dallas* connoisseurs, offering the story of Miss Ellie and Jock's romance, the Barnes-Ewing feud origins, and shots of the formative Bobby-J.R. rivalry.

6
Dynasty –
Long Live the Queen

To recall the origins of the programme that made soaps essential cult viewing, we must go back to the stone age before the name Alexis meant anything, back when Joan Collins was a minor actress, back in those dreary days when John Forsythe could walk the streets without being recognised.

In this primeval era, soap operas were considered housewife fodder in America. They glutted the working hours from 10 a.m. to 4 p.m. but vanished before most of the middle class came home to watch sitcoms, movies and 'serious' drama.

ABC, the youngest of the three US networks, had enjoyed success with a prime-time evening soap in the 1960s, *Peyton Place*. Because it launched stars such as Ryan O'Neal and Mia Farrow, and because it was loosely based on 'literature' (the Grace Metalious novels), *Peyton Place* was seen as a quality series. Cancelled in the 1960s, it was not immediately replaced with anything similar.

But in the mid–1970s, ABC began tampering with the soap formula again, producing a hybrid called the mini-series, which ran for a set number of episodes (and was generally based on a novel), but otherwise featured the continuing plots, subplots and romance of a good soap. *Rich Man, Poor Man*, a twelve-hour entry based on an Irwin Shaw novel about two brothers loving, feuding and scheming from World War II to the 1960s, sprang to the top of the ratings. ABC's *Roots*, a better and more important tale of black heritage, based on Alex Haley's book, smashed ratings records.

It was a winning formula with a problem. Expensive to produce, these mini-series turned major profits for the network, but filled a limited block of time (usually twelve hours) and were basically one-shot telecasts. CBS, by expanding its own mini-series *Dallas* into a continuing series (as would have been tacky with, say, *Roots*), found a way to combine the mini-series cliffhangers and popularity with the extended run of a dramatic series.

In doing so CBS had, of course, merely created a night-time soap, albeit a hugely expensive one. Not to be outdone at its own game, ABC decided to create an even bigger night-time soap, a lush continuing drama with the production values and star names of a film. Executives aproached Esther and Richard Shapiro, authors of such gritty TV movies as *Sarah T, Portrait of a Teenage Alcoholic*.

Their brief was straightforward: ABC wanted sex, drama, gloss, beautiful women, powerful men. Forget believability – this family should be not only larger than life, but larger than fiction too. It all boiled down to '*Dallas* Plus'. Producing this exercise in conspicuous consumption would be Aaron Spelling, whose production credits included such slick numbers as *Charlie's Angels*, *The Love Boat* and *Heart to Heart*. Spelling had produced a soap-style programme, *Family*, from 1976 to 1980.

Just Your Average Billionaires

The Shapiros fashioned the family next door – if you happen to live next door to the Rockefellers. The Carringtons would live in Denver, in a forty-eight room mansion from which the men would buy and sell financial empires while the women would sashay around in television's most expensive gowns. Their business was oil, just like the Ewings, thus the series' sparkling original title, *Oil*. It was changed to *Dynasty* because *Oil* sounded too much like a second-rate *Dallas* (whereas the programme was second-generation *Dallas*).

The big man, Jock Ewing puffed and buffed to a fine sheen, was Blake Carrington, patriarch extraordinaire, president of the oil firm Denver Carrington, flanked by his two children, honest, proud, bisexual Steven and beautiful, spoiled Fallon. Handsome Jeff Colby would marry Fallon, the object of his adoration. Blake would wed his secretary, all-American beauty Krystle Grant Jennings, in episode one. It was all too grand and glorious for words.

The fantastic sets for the Carrington mansion were based on Filoli, an actual house in San Mateo, California, with forty-eight rooms and seventeen working fireplaces. Like the real Southfork ranch used in *Dallas*, this home has become a tourist attraction.

While set designers copied Filoli, casting began for the principals. George Peppard, a successful film actor and star of the series *Banacek*, didn't fancy a soap and rejected the Blake role (he later turned up lobbing grenades in *The A Team*). Spelling then called on John Forsythe, the voice of Charlie in *Charlie's Angels* and the visual epitome of a distinguished gentleman, who accepted.

John James fancied the Steven role but producers couldn't see him as a bisexual, so the Jeff Colby role was created for him. Steven went to Al Corley, with lovely Pamela Sue Martin picked for Fallon. Finally, Linda Evans, old enough to seem motherly but still a representation of American glamour, made a perfect Krystle.

A three-hour television movie announced *Dynasty* to the world. Having spent more on their sets and costumes than *Dallas*, and with a winning group of actors, ABC expected

Joan Collins who plays Alexis in Dynasty.

Dynasty to knock *Dallas* out of the top-rated positions. It didn't. The series premiered on 12 January 1981 in the States, to good but not astounding ratings. What was wrong?

Enter Her Majesty

Hindsight makes it easy to see that *Dynasty* had left out the special ingredient that made *Dallas* so tasty: evil. The Carringtons were incredibly powerful and incredibly good. Challengers to Blake's throne of wisdom and strength flailed about like pesky gnats. The first season's cliffhanger, involving Blake being accused of murdering his son's gay lover, lacked suspense: who could really hope to bring down this majestic man?

Who indeed? Top soap writers Eileen and Robert Pollack came to the series in its second season and introduced many intriguing plot twists, none so successful as the introduction of Blake's ex-wife, a femme fatale without the strong moral convictions that were boring viewers. Producer Aaron Spelling sought out Sophia Loren for the part, but the Italian actress just wasn't interested. With little time before the cliffhanger's shooting dates, Spelling remembered working on *The Making of a Male Model* with British star Joan Collins.

67

Her fiery dark looks and clipped voice had landed Joan many bitch roles in the past, but here was her chance to go for broke. Expecting no more than a season's work, Joan took the part. From her first dramatic appearance in the courtroom, she had the *Dynasty* audience eating out of her hand, and the *Dynasty* characters watching their backs.

Joan's show-stopping portrayal of Alexis turned *Dynasty*'s fortunes around. J.R. was nasty, but Jock Ewing could slap him into line now and again. Unfettered, Alexis wreaked havoc whilst maintaining her seductive attraction. Alexis fused every man's sexual fantasy with the castration fear, while managing to look thirty-five as she approached fifty. Huge homosexual followings worshipped her, and before long *Dynasty* was required viewing for the hip, a cultural icon for the upwardly mobile 1980s.

A Tale of Empire

Dynasty commences when Blake marries Krystle Grant Jennings, his secretary. Blake's daughter Fallon is soon found naked in their swimming pool with Jeff Colby. Steven, Blake's son, has a gay affair with Ted Dinard. Not to be outdone, Fallon switches to Michael, the chauffeur. Cecil Colby, Blake's rival and Jeff's uncle, agrees to help Blake financially if Jeff marries Fallon – he does, in Las Vegas.

Blake's good fortune quickly wanes. Catching Steven and Ted hugging, Blake hits Ted, who strikes his head and dies. At the trial, where Blake is found guilty of involuntary manslaughter, the surprise witness is his ex-wife Alexis Carrington, who tells the court Blake is an evil man and cruelly sent her away during their marriage. Alexis then moves into her old studio flat in the mansion grounds. On probation, Blake rapes Krystle and goes temporarily blind. He soon reconciles with his wife.

Steve plays the other half of the field and marries Krystle's niece, Sammy Jo. Cecil Colby double-crosses Blake and calls in the loan. The Blaisdels show up: Claudia, Matthew and their daughter Lindsay. Matthew works for Blake on the Denver oil wells. Claudia spends time in a mental home and testifies that she was Steven's lover at the time of Dinard's murder. Matthew flees this

revelation with Lindsay, and they are believed to be killed in South America. Steven leaves Denver after announcing he is definitely gay.

Alexis, meanwhile, has set herself up as ruler of the roost, making life tough for Steven and Sammy Jo, whose marriage she abhors, and for Krystle, with whom she has periodic battles (in an apartment, in a pool, in a beauty salon). When Krystle finds she's pregnant, Alexis 'accidentally' fires a gun as Krystle is riding. The horse bolts and Krystle loses the child. Fallon, who has learned she may be Cecil Colby's daughter, loses her newborn son Blake to kidnappers, but soon gets him back.

When the Carringtons make a television appeal for the return of Blake Junior, an old woman in Billings, Montana sees it and tells her grandson Michael Torrance he is the Carringtons' long-lost son who was kidnapped as a baby by Kate Torrance! Indeed, Blake and Alexis had lost a child, Adam, to kidnappers in 1955.

Michael Torrance shows up in Denver to claim his birthright and the Carringtons take him in. Drugs have soured him, though, and he tries to kill Jeff and put the blame on Alexis. Undaunted, Alexis marries Cecil Colby on his deathbed, thereby inheriting his oil firm, Colbyco, with which she can wage war on Blake.

Steven goes missing when the South-east Asia oil rig he is working on explodes. He is later found in a Singapore hospital with a new face. Sammy Jo shows up with her baby, Danny, Steven's baby. Jeff and Fallon's marriage breaks up. Alexis and Fallon have a brief affair with Mark Jennings, Krystle's ex-husband, then Alexis hires him as her bodyguard. Alexis and Krystle are trapped in a burning cabin and rescued by Mark – after he dies Alexis is accused of the murder.

Krystle has learned she was never legally divorced from Jennings, which puts a strain on her marriage to Blake and they separate. Blake brings a suit against Steven for custody of Danny since Steven is living with

Linda Evans (Krystle Carrington), John Forsythe (Blake Carrington) and Pam Sue Martin (the 'old' Fallon).

his lover/lawyer Chris Deegan. Steven retains Danny by marrying Claudia.

Fallon meets drug dealer Peter De Vilbus. When she discovers he's a con man, he runs over her, temporarily paralysing her. She and Jeff get back together but, on their wedding day, she vanishes. Everyone assumes Fallon has run off to De Vilbus, and that she has died when De Vilbus's plane goes down.

It's wedding bells again for Blake and Krystle, though, who remarry (legally this time, since Mark is dead) and find Krystle can have children after all. Their daughter Kristina, is born. Chic Dominique appears, claiming to be Blake's sister by Blake's father, who confirms the story on his deathbed. With her comes Brady Lloyd, her husband.

Alexis, convicted of murdering Jennings, marries Dex Dexter and escapes her rap when Mark's killer is revealed to be congressman Neal McVane. Another lost Carrington surfaces: Amanda, Blake and Alexis's youngest, who Blake never knew about. She becomes engaged to Prince Michael of Moldavia, but enemy terrorists later ruin the ceremony in Moldavia with a massacre.

Jeff has an affair with De Vilbus's widow, then becomes the lover of Lady Ashley Mitchell. Blake suspects Krystle is having an affair with Daniel Reece, her sister's old boyfriend and Sammy Jo's father, whose estate Sammy Jo inherits when Daniel dies. Steven and Claudia break up when Steven meets Luke Fuller, who dies at the Moldavia wedding. Sammy Jo gets her friend Rita to masquerade as Krystle, the executrix of Daniel Reece's will, but the ruse is found out.

Adam marries Claudia, who is killed in the fire at La Mirage. Dominique supports Blake when Alexis buys Blake's debts from his creditors and calls them in. The result leaves Blake bankrupt – Alexis even takes the house.

Blake's long-lost brother Ben is found by Alexis. Amanda and Sammy Jo fall in love with Clay, but Sammy Jo marries him. Amanda falls for Michael, the former chauffeur, long since banished and now returned as a businessman out to get even with Blake.

More relatives drop in: Alexis's sister Caress, released from a South American jail, and Ben Carrington's daughter Leslie.

Amanda heads for London, Sammy Jo divorces Clay and goes after Steven again, leaving Clay to woo Leslie, who could be his half sister. Kristina falls ill and needs a new heart. Adam learns he's not Adam after all, but Michael Torrance! Blake and Alexis adopt him, but at his wedding the house is stormed by Matthew Blaisdel, alive after all, who kidnaps most of the family, including ex-friend Steven and would-be lover Krystle. Steven causes Matthew's death and must search his soul.

Alexis is saved from drowning in a car by a stranger, Sean. She soon marries him in a quick Mexican ceremony. Meanwhile, Jeff has found Fallon (whom he remarried on *The Colbys* after her marriage to Miles Colby, and who vanished on a desert drive), who claims to have been abducted by beings from another world. But have the aliens done anything to her?

Filming the Series

With their ratings success assured, Spelling and the Shapiros have honed their formula and spent production fortunes with confidence. *Dynasty* costs approximately one million dollars per episode, with the minimum clothes budget at $25,000.

Behind the scenes, hard work replaces glamour. The show is filmed in two massive concrete buildings in the vast Warner Hollywood studios, stages 3, 4 and 5. Each stage measures 200 ft × 100 ft, housing cavernous offices, drawing rooms, staircases and reception areas. Shooting an episode takes seven days, with another four weeks allotted for editing, polishing, reshoots, etc. It may look as if the actors' lives consist largely of swanning about in fashionable homes, but the truth is far more uncomfortable. Though the studios are air-conditioned against California's often sweltering heat, the air-conditioning makes too much noise, and must be switched off during filming. Heavy suits and dresses weigh the poor actors down as they struggle through retakes, in temperatures reaching the nineties. This heat notwithstanding, the flowers seen in the Carrington mansion are not plastic or paper, but are delivered fresh daily.

A *Dynasty* working day begins at 6 a.m. for the crew, who rig sets and lighting, and at 7 a.m. for the stars. Even Joan Collins and Linda Evans must clock in with their own time-cards – not because they're paid by the hour but to keep track of who's there. The women have an hour to be made up, the men half an hour. Despite their large salaries and fan clubs, stars aren't pampered, as the *Dynasty* shooting schedules are rigid.

The Moldavia Massacre and Other Highlights

Out-Dallasing *Dallas* meant more than just letting supershrew Alexis do her stuff. With their sights set on the 'Who shot J.R.?' storyline, the Shapiros and Pollacks set out to create the world's greatest cliffhanger in the 1984/5 season, set in the mythical land of Moldavia.

Alexis had engineered a royal wedding between her youngest daughter, Amanda, and Prince Michael of Moldavia. She shipped most of the Carrington clan to Moldavia for the wedding. Unknown to her, the country's underground planned to usurp the regime of King Galen by bumping off the royal family and much of the *Dynasty* cast, whose contracts were up for renewal. This would make the country a republic and enable the scriptwriters to skim off a few extraneous characters while pumping up the series' ratings.

Dex Dexter was kidnapped before the wedding when he learned what was planned. He escaped prior to the bloodbath and rushed to the wedding, hoping to avert disaster. But he was too late. Amidst the rubble of the ruined church were most of the Carringtons and company, dusty and bloody – but no Alexis.

For a well-planned terrorist massacre, a surprising number of the victims limped their way into the 1985/6 season. In fact, when the dust cleared, only two characters didn't get up: Luke Fuller and Lady Ashley Mitchell. Actress Ali McGraw knew she was headed for extinction when the make-up woman applying fake blood to her was told, 'More blood! More blood!' And as for Luke (William Campbell), well, Steven's male lovers have notoriously short lifespans.

Where was Alexis? Actually, she, or rather Joan Collins, was renegotiating her contract as filming began. Once she and the producers were satisfied, she showed up in the third episode of the new season, when it was revealed that Alexis had been held prisoner during the siege.

Notable though the episode before the massacre was, the final appearances of Rock Hudson (as Daniel Reece) proved to be the high point of the 1984/5 season. A leading sex symbol for three decades, Rock succumbed to AIDS in 1985, provoking gossip-mongering in the tabloids, including speculation that he had passed AIDS on to Linda Evans during their love scenes. This was nonsense, of course, and rightly annoyed those who mourned the great actor.

Even more thrilling than Matthew's dramatic 1987 siege was the real-life terror that ensued when Alexis married her life-saver, Sean (James Healey). Insiders say Joan Collins thought the wedding was a bit too soon, but the producers wanted to improve the ratings. Joan was destined to remember forever her fourth *Dynasty* wedding day: the scene was just beginning on the morning of 1 October 1987, when the entire Hollywood sound-stage began to rumble and shake.

Joan escaped the building, followed by the rest of the cast and crew as a major earthquake rocked Los Angeles. The tremor, measuring around 6.0 on the Richter scale, knocked down sets and delayed shooting for two hours. Joan allegedly saw it as an omen that she was right and Alexis shouldn't marry so soon, but she was persuaded to finish the wedding scene.

Kings and Queens

He's Mr Nice Guy for the camera, and behind it too. John Forsythe is described as a 'perfect gentleman' by *Dynasty*'s cast and crew. John, who lives with his wife of forty-two years, Julie, and their poodle Angel in the Hollywood Hills, starred in the first TV-movie, *See How They Run*, in 1965, and has been seen in such films as 1979's *And Justice for All*, where he played a perverted judge.

One of *Dynasty*'s older generation, John has survived a quadruple-bypass heart operation, and today plays tennis to keep fit for twelve-hour shooting days. His concern

over the problems of age led him to produce a recent TV film *Fired*, in which he plays a man forced to retire at sixty.

John feels a responsibility to portray Blake in an upright, consistent fashion, and put his foot down when the writers called for him to dally with Lady Ashley (Ali MacGraw). John insisted Blake would never take up with another woman, and forced the writers into a compromise whereby the two hovered on the verge of an affair that fizzled.

'*Dynasty* is the dramatised fantasy of every middle-aged woman,' says Esther Shapiro, and besides Blake one major factor is Linda Evans. As Krystle, Linda has set new standards for middle-aged beauty, breaking the 'mother' stereotype that dogs actresses in their forties. No aprons or old print dresses for this woman, thank you – Linda has helped bring shoulder pads back into fashion, and women around the world seek out the Krystle look when shopping.

The victim of two bad marriages, to John Derek (who left her for Bo after seventeen years) and property developer Stan Herman, Linda is quite happy to stay single, though it has meant abandoning her chances of having a baby. She has passed the safe age now, and found it difficult to deal with playing a pregnant Krystle in the series; she's often teary eyed when holding little Jessica. In fact, Linda had an abortion at age seventeen, after being seduced by a fairground worker.

Her recent TV appearances include *The Gambler* with singer Kenny Rogers, *The Last Frontier* and *North and South 2*. Linda is clearly trying to broaden her image, and has suggested that she will leave *Dynasty* in the near future, perhaps followed by John Forsythe and/or Joan Collins.

Unlike rival no-good J.R. and Larry Hagman, Alexis and Joan are virtually synonymous. The two women may be very different, but try telling that to fans who soak up stories about Joan's four marriages and luxurious shopping sprees. Joan bolstered her image with the Peter Holm divorce, which brought into the public eye her wealth and temper, and made headlines of questionable quotes like, 'I'll never let a

The very glamorous Linda Evans who plays Blake's wife Krystle.

man rule me again!' Spoken like the real Alexis Morell Carrington Colby Dexter.

She wasn't born a star, but it didn't take her long to become one. Her father, Joe Collins, ran a theatrical agency with Lew Grade, later head of ATV. Accepted to RADA in her teens, Joan went from modelling to a role as a juvenile delinquent in *I Believe in You* with Celia Johnson. Only nineteen, her career took off and she married film star Maxwell Reed – for a month.

Promoting *Road to Hong Kong* with Bob Hope and Bing Crosby, Joan met Anthony Newley in London and married him in 1963. The couple had two children, Tara and Alexander, during their seven-year marriage. In 1972 she married Ron Kass, by whom she had Katyana before the divorce in 1984. Her most recent marriage began when she met Peter Holm, a former Swedish pop singer. He moved into Joan's Hollywood home and

John Forsythe (Blake) with his off-screen wife Julie.

73

the couple formed a production company for TV mini-series such as *Sins* and *Monte Carlo*. Their wedding photos provoked a legal battle between the *News of the World* and the US's *National Enquirer*: both published the photos but the *Enquirer* claims to have paid $160,000 for the exclusive rights. Joan and Peter divorced on the front-page of the papers, every indictment and insult a headline.

Chronicling the ups and downs of Joan's career has taken several biographies, so suffice to say that she'd fallen on hard times when best-selling sister Jackie offered a film project called *The Stud*. This and its sort-of sequel *The Bitch* paid the bills (as had horror films like *Tales From the Crypt* and *Empire of the Ants*) until *Dynasty* transformed her into a superstar. Her post-*Dynasty* offerings such as *Sins* may be schlock but they're expensive schlock, and she now has the luxury of co-producing her vehicles.

Women lust after him . . . and so do men. As bisexual Steven Carrington, Jack Coleman has a mixed-gender adoration society and cult-hero status among those who worship fave 'fag hag' Alexis. But there probably isn't much of Steven in Jack, who spends much of his time with long-term steady Christine Kellogg. A cagey Jack says only that he and Steven are identical in both wanting to be liked.

Jack took over the role in 1982 after Al Corley's departure. Al, who had rowed with the producers over the series' content, later featured in the 1985 film *Torchlight*, starring its co-author and producer, Pamela Sue Martin. The film was a brief reunion for the two *Dynasty* expatriates.

Awful Adam Carrington generally plays the bad boy. He once tried to kill Jeff Colby and blame it on his mother, he has had a serious drug problem, tried to double-cross his father and isn't even sure whether the Carringtons are his parents. Gordon Thomson can relate, having had his share of mixed-up moments too. Most of his pre-*Dynasty* acting career involved struggling to avoid debt collectors between roles. This took the young Gordon to the brink of suicide until he learned that such a drastic step would delay his heirs receiving the money.

A genius with an IQ of 154, Gordon attended a prestigious private school and Montreal's McGill University. He has worked for the Canadian Broadcasting Company, an American soap opera, and has also been married to Irish actress Maureen Fitzgerald. In 1987 Gordon had a regular spot on ITV's breakfast station, TV AM.

Fortunately, unlike Adam, Gordon is a sensitive fellow. Otherwise, he could easily spook Leann Hunley, who was at first terrified of her bed scenes with Gordon. Leann suffered 'sheet shock' after a bad experience on the daytime soap *Days of Our Lives*, when her partner in a love scene whispered 'I have no underpants on.' A shocked Leann leapt screaming from the bed, spoiling the take – a taboo on the time-pressured daily soaps.

A former Miss Hawaii, Leann took part-time jobs before winning roles in *Hawaii Five-O* and *Days of Our Lives*. The demands of a five-day shooting schedule for the latter made her ask for time off in order to enjoy life with her husband, Bill Sheridan. When the producers refused, she walked out and into the *Dynasty* cast, where her screen time is less and retakes are permitted.

Once a male model, Ted McGinley was noticeably stiff in his role as Roger in the *Happy Days* series, and was doubtless cast for his suave face alone in *The Making of a Male Model*. But that film, produced by Aaron Spelling and starring Joan Collins, led to his joining the *Dynasty* cast, where he's honed his acting skills as studly Clay Fallmont. Lucky Ted now spends much of his time in the arms of glamorous women such as Catherine Oxenberg (Amanda), Terri Garber (Leslie) and Heather Locklear (Sammy Jo). Whereas many actors bleach their hair, Ted dyes his blonde locks darker so as not to clash with Jack Coleman. He spends part of his summer at a Malibu camp for children with cancer.

To media-watchers, Heather Locklear is a triple-threat star. She's steamy Sammy Jo on *Dynasty*, Stacy Sheridan on the erstwhile *TJ Hooker* with William Shatner, and the real-life wife of Tommy Lee, member of the controversial heavy metal rock group Motley Crue. With her California beach-bunny looks, Heather still wasn't sure she could make it as an actress when she dropped

Jack Coleman who plays Blake's bi-sexual son, Steven Carrington.

(whom she nearly married, but for Frost's disinclination to leave London) and Sidney Poitier, she has been married to four men.

Diahann is now happily married to international star Vic Damone. Before their January 1987 wedding, Joan Collins threw the bridal shower, and presented a racy gift of expensive underwear. Vic spent their honeymoon in hospital with kidney stones, but the two have a happy marriage, and appeared together live on London Weekend TV in April 1987.

With John James's departure for *The Colbys*, Michael Nader became *Dynasty*'s reigning pin-up as Dex Dexter. Michael maintains the series moves faster than *Dallas* or *Knots Landing* and has more emotion: the sizzle when he and Joan Collins meet, he says, shows in the electric scenes between Dex and Alexis.

Drugs nearly kept Michael from the small screen until film production assistant Robin Weiss, now his wife, turned his life around and his acting career took an upturn. Their daughter Lindsey Michelle was the victim of a kidnap threat after Michael's *Dynasty* fame;

Ted McGinley, once a male model, plays Dynasty's *desirable Clay Fallmont.*

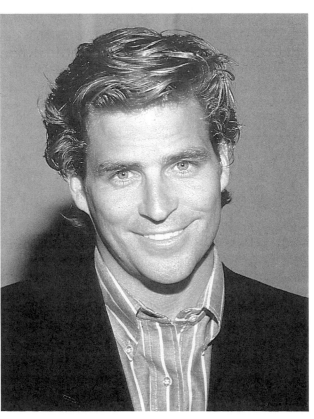

out of psychology major in college. She attended acting classes with a friend who didn't want to go alone, then made commercials before being signed to *two* major series. During her time on *Dynasty* and *TJ Hooker*, she split the week between the two shows.

It *is* hard to find good help these days, so hard that after Michael, the Carringtons' chauffeur, was banished for his affair with Fallon, he bounced back for the 1986/7 season. Wayne Northrop was glad to return to prime time after his period as Roman Brady on the daytime soap *Days of Our Lives*. Wayne says he looks up to John Forsythe but doesn't look forward to his love scenes: 'The last thing on your mind is sex when you have lights, cameramen and directors all around you.'

Diahann Carroll, so wicked as Dominique Deveraux, had her own series in the 1960s. The comedy-drama series *Julia*, in which she played a single mother and nurse, was basically a vehicle for her formidable talent. Diahann has also had a prominent singing career, and a string of well-publicised romances. Besides affairs with David Frost

Christopher Cazenove (Ben Carrington), Blake's 'long lost' brother and Joan Collins (Alexis).

armed guards and a gun under Michael's pillow were safeguards against intruders who never materialised. Incidentally, a drunk's reckless driving left six-year-old Michael with a broken arm . . . and daring Dex's scar.

Christopher Cazenove got a chance to star in his family's favourite show when Aaron Spelling cast him as Ben Carrington, Blake's 'long-lost' brother. He and his family moved to Beverly Hills, where Christopher's instalment of *This Is Your Life* would later be filmed. When his marriage to actress Angharad Rees faltered, Christopher moved out but continued to see their children, Linford and 'Rhys William. He and Angharad were reunited when Christopher made *Lace II*, and took a second honeymon to Thailand.

Long-lost brother Ben found on *Dynasty* his long-lost daughter Leslie Carrington (Terri Garber), whom he left in Australia but who speaks with an American accent. She must really have been lost! A former model, Terri Garber met technician Chris Hayer on the set of the Civil War mini-series *North and South*, and the couple now have a daughter, Molly. Her role as vixen Aston Maine in *North and South* also served as her 'audition' for *Dynasty*.

While on the subject of family matters, Alexis's imprisoned sister, Cassandra Caress Morell, has also turned up. For actress Kate O'Mara, *Dynasty* is quite a switch from her earlier soap experience on *Triangle*, which involved sailing the North Sea during the treacherous autumn months. Herself a good sailor, Kate would often be green with sea-sickness, and once found her make-up girl lying on the cabin floor being ill. Kate saw to the girl, then made herself up for the day's shots.

After experiences like that, Kate was mortified to find herself being coated in make-up for *Dynasty* shots. The make-up department would lay it on with a trowel even when Cassandra could be forgiven for not looking her best. For realism's sake, Kate once demanded to make herself up for the prison scene – the producers agreed and Kate's *au naturel* look went down fine.

Kate and Joan Collins had been stablemates at Pinewood Studios in the 1960s, and find working together on *Dynasty* a bit like old times. Like Joan, Kate's private life has been duly noted in the press. She put her son Dixon up for adoption after the divorce from his father, but was recently reunited with him. Also, like Joan, she goes for (gasp!) younger men, and lived until recently with Leslie Howard's grandson Steven, ten years her junior.

Sitting Pretty

Like the best of the soaps, *Dynasty* has had its internal squabbles. The latest and biggest saw Aaron Spelling putting his shares in his production company on the market in 1986. Cited as assets of the production company were *Dynasty* and *The Colbys*. The Shapiros, claiming they own 40 per cent of both those series, put a block on the sale and sued Spelling.

Despite such competition among its creators, *Dynasty* no longer needs to worry about rival *Dallas*. Alexis and company steadily outstrip J.R.'s Texans in popularity, and sit securely on the throne as the world's most popular soap opera. And there *Dynasty* will probably remain, at least until Alexis goes soft . . . which means contenders have a long, long wait ahead.

Dynasty Runaways – The Colbys

After *Dallas*'s successful spin-off, *Dynasty* producers felt they could siphon off some of the show's population explosion into another programme. Thus, 1985 saw the

Blake tried to strangle his ex-wife Alexis, after she won his mansion from him.

debut of *The Colbys* (originally *Dynasty 2: The Colbys*), as Jeff Colby went to live in Los Angeles with his relations.

His surprise co-star was Fallon, seemingly back from the dead. When last seen, Fallon had been ready to remarry Jeff after her brief fling with shady Peter De Vilbus (Helmut Berger, famed European star of *The Damned* and other films). But she disappeared before tying the knot with Jeff, and when De Vilbus's plane crashed, two bodies were found, along with Fallon's ring.

But as *The Colbys*'s plot-line explained, Fallon had not been aboard De Vilbus's plane. After driving off in a dangerous storm before her proposed wedding to Jeff, Fallon, stricken with head pains, had developed amnesia. She had wandered lost through the USA, unable to find her way back to *Dynasty*'s prime-time spot. Calling herself Randall Adams, she had eventually seen a story about Miles Colby and sought him out in

Los Angeles, marrying him. Jeff was only too happy to sort out these tangled lines now that he had his Fallon back.

Even after Jeff had remarried Fallon, things would never be easy with her. As *The Colbys* reached the end of its two-year run, one of soap's most peculiar plots unfolded when Fallon was kidnapped by aliens from outer space! Highly reminiscent of the comedy series *Soap*, which featured alien impregnations and impersonations, the

story-line saw Fallon driving down to the Mexican border to save her mother-in-law Frankie, who had been kidnapped by her ex-husband Philip.

When her car stalled on the deserted highway, Fallon got out and saw a spaceship landing. Mesmerised by its brilliant lights, she was hailed by one of its strange occupants and taken on board. When she mysteriously reappeared on *Dynasty* at the start of the 1987/8 season, she had a hard time convincing Jeff of her experience. After describing her examination by needles on board the craft, she said the ship smelt of cinnamon. 'I see,' Jeff quipped. 'Were they baking?'

The Colbys' Cast

Actress Pamela Sue Martin wasn't interested in coming back, though, so for *The Colbys* Fallon's visage somehow transformed into that of the no-less-lovely Emma Samms, a former ballet dancer, model and medical technician. Emma made her mark on the popular us daytime soap *General Hospital* as Holly Sutton, a Briton who romanced both the series' male leads, Luke and Scorpio (Anthony Geary and Tristan Rogers).

But the mundane manoeuvres of daytime TV hadn't prepared her for *Dynasty*'s eccentricities. Before joining *The Colbys* in L.A., Emma went through some cameos on *Dynasty*. Her first appearance was in a flashback with John James (to convince startled viewers that Fallon had always looked like Emma?). She says the two, slated for a long screen relationship, had no introduction before the scene began: 'We just said hi, then went into this kiss.'

Society gossips have always called Emma stuck-up and have even slighted her acting ability, but the real-life Fallon is a generous woman who works with Starlight, an organisation that arranges special outings and gifts for dying children. In this, Emma joins such luminaries as Michael Jackson and Elizabeth Taylor.

Once dubbed by Joan Collins 'the prettiest person on the show', John James has blossomed into more than just a sex symbol, though he's still pursued by legions of female

The 'new' Fallon in Dynasty – *Emma Samms.*

fans. Formerly a student at the American
Academy of Dramatic Arts in New York,
John worked on *Search for Tomorrow*, a
daytime soap, before auditioning to be
Steven Carrington, and winding up as Jeff
Colby. Back then in a second banana role,
Jeff Colby moved into the spotlight more
and more before spearheading *The Colbys*.
Since then he has stepped out on his own in
the television movies *He's Not Your Son*,
where he co-starred with Donna Mills of
Knots Landing.

*John James (Jeff Colby) with his girlfriend Marcia
Wolfe.*

Attention from amorous women may
sound fun to some guys, but it grew to be a
headache for John when he started getting
late-night calls from strange girls, something
his girlfriend Marcia Wolfe didn't appreciate. To prove his fidelity, John announced to
Joan Rivers and her national audience on *The
Tonight Show* that he and Marcia were
engaged.

79

When he signed on for *The Colbys*, Charlton Heston was the biggest name in soaps and a casting coup for producer Spelling. The recipient of a best-actor Oscar in 1959 for *Ben Hur*, Charlton is also famous for such roles as Moses in *The Ten Commandments*. He had script control over Jason Colby's actions and dialogue (virtually unheard-of for an actor) and, with Barbara Stanwyck, gave the series a greater air of respectability.

An arch conservative and long-time friend of Ronald Reagan's, Charlton clashed with Edward Asner and other liberals in the Screen Actors Guild, and formed the right-wing breakaway group Actors Working for an Actors Guild. Since *The Colbys* he has pursued his political career, starred in *Proud Men* for American television and appeared on the London stage in *A Man for All Seasons*.

During his stint on the show, the wrath of Heston fell on Maxwell Caulfield, the bad boy of the cast who plays Miles Colby. Barbara Stanwyck refused to do some scenes with Maxwell, and a split-screen technique was used so that the actors could film separately. Charlton defended Barbara and wrote an angry letter to Maxwell, demanding that he clean up his act.

Born in Derbyshire and raised in London, Maxwell isn't the all-American mischief maker he seems. He went to the States in his teens and landed the starring role in *Grease 2* – when the original *Grease* film opened at London's Leicester Square Odeon, Maxwell had been a ticket collector in the theatre. Before becoming Miles Colby, Maxwell also played in a roadshow of *The Elephant Man*, where he met his future wife, British actress Juliet Mills, twenty years his senior.

The confused woman-child of *The Graduate* with Dustin Hoffman, Katharine Ross has played romantic leads opposite some of Hollywood's handsomest men, including both Robert Redford and Paul Newman in *Butch Cassidy and the Sundance Kid*. For *The Colbys* she emerged from semi-retirement for a different kind of part: the mother of Jeff Colby, Francesca Scott Colby Hamilton. Not only does Katharine look too young to have borne John James, she *is* too young. She was forty-three when the series was cast, while John was twenty-nine!

Another top Hollywood star recruited for the series was Barbara Stanwyck, who played Constance Colby Patterson. Born Ruby Stevens in 1907, Barbara's film career spanned some eighty-four films, from classics such as *Double Indemnity* and *Clash By Night* to more modern outings such as the television production *The Thorn Birds*.

Bliss Colby always had a slight English accent, not because the part demands it, but because lovely Clare Yarlett was educated at an English convent school. Clare was picked by producers after an extensive search for a girl beautiful enough to be the youngest

daughter of Sable and Jason. They admired her performance as Dakota Lane in the *Dynasty*-like television production *Rituals*.

Suave Mexico-born Ricardo Montalban starred in *The Latin Lover* in the 1950s and has many films under his belt, but since the 1980s has been known chiefly as Tattoo's boss in *Fantasy Island*. He once dreamed of becoming a matador, but found a safer life in acting. Apart from Zack Powers, Ricardo's fans have seen him as an ultra-villain in *Star Trek II: The Wrath of Khan*.

After failing to make the US diving team in 1980, Tracy Scoggins turned to acting and

The wedding that never was. Katherine Ross (Francesca) and Charlton Heston (Jason).

was soon cast as brainy Monica Colby. Texas-born Tracy believes in clean living and extols the virtues taught to her by her late father: no smoking, no drugs and no drinking. No wonder Tracy manages to avoid the scandal sheets.

Living next door to Tracy in Malibu was co-star Stephanie Beacham. A RADA graduate, Stephanie has worked in television, theatre and film, has starred in *The Nightcomers* with Marlon Brando, an ITV

Maxwell Caulfield (Miles Colby) and Kim Morgan Greene.

series *Marked Personal*, Central TV's series *Connie*, and the BBC's *Tenko*. Recently she has returned to the stage in Aphra Behn's *The Rover*. While making *Tenko*, Stephanie was rescued from a severe bout of anorexia by a fellow actor, who forced her back into healthy eating patterns.

Stephanie's children Phoebe and Chloe attended boarding school in England while their mother earned their tuition on *The Colbys*, which gave her the chance to play opposite her hero Charlton Heston as his wife. Even to observant viewers, her handicap is invisible: Stephanie is deaf in one ear and partially deaf in the other, relying largely on lip reading to understand others.

Is Fallon Pregnant with E.T.?

Despite *The Colbys'* cancellation, its stronger story-lines live on in *Dynasty*. One writers' faction at *Dynasty* has fought to exploit tabloid-style 'Fallon's Flying Saucer' plot by having Fallon become pregnant – the big question being, 'Will Fallon bear a space baby?' Another *Dynasty* faction considers the whole sci-fi story completely over-the-top, and would like to get back to some good, honest cheating and scheming stories. Whichever side wins, the future looks rocky for Jeff and his high-flying wife.

Dynasty

First episode credits:
Transmitted 12 January, 1981 in US,
   1 May, 1982 in UK.
Produced by Aaron Spelling
Created by Richard and Esther Shapiro
An Aaron Spelling Production for the
   ABC TV Network

Original Cast List

Character	Actor
Blake Carrington	John Forsythe
Krystle Carrington	Linda Evans
Fallon Carrington	Pamela Sue Martin
Steven Carrington	Al Corley
Cecil Colby	Lloyd Bochner
Jeff Colby	John James
Joseph Anders	Lee Begere
Matthew Blaisdel	Bo Hopkins
Claudia Blaisdel	Pamela Bellwood
Lindsay Blaisdel	Kathy Kurtzman
Walter Lankershim	Dale Robertson
Michael Culhan	Wayne Northrop

The Colbys

First episode credits:
Transmitted 20 November, 1985 in US,
   24 January 1986 in UK.
Produced by Aaron Spelling
Created by Richard and Esther Shapiro
An Aaron Spelling Production for the
   ABC TV Network

Original Cast List

Character	Actor
Jason Colby	Charlton Heston
Jeff Colby	John James
Francesca Scott Colby Hamilton	Katherine Ross
Fallon Carrington Colby	Emma Samms
Miles Colby	Maxwell Caulfield
Sable Colby	Stephanie Beacham
Monica Colby	Tracy Scoggins
Hutch	Joseph Campanella
Bliss Colby	Clare Yarlett
Zack Powers	Ricardo Montalban
Garret Boydson	Ken Howard
Constance Colby Patterson	Barbara Stanwyck

7
Brookside –
The Thinking Person's Soap

When Channel 4 burst on to the airwaves in 1982 like a blast of fresh air, it brought with it a programme that blew away the tired conventions and flimsy stucco sets of the soap opera genre. BBC 1 and 2 and ITV, the triumvirate of television, had ruled the airwaves for decades, time enough to become old-fogies, and their children had aged as well – even *Crossroads* had turned eighteen in 1982. Young television writer Phil Redmond sought to create a new kid on the block – one that could go where no soap had gone before.

Redmond, a former quantity surveyor, had already authored many scripts when the BBC picked up his idea for the children's soap *Grange Hill* in 1976. Redmond's life in the settled regions of the television upper echelon was set as *Grange Hill* succeeded, spawning the Redmond-written *Tucker's Luck* and leading to *County Hall* (BBC) and *Going Out* (Southern TV) for the young man.

But the teen rebel in Redmond kicked against the bureaucratic thinking of the big TV corporations, and the fledgling Channel 4 caught his fancy. Why languish in writing for others when he could create shows for a new network? Redmond formed Mersey TV and took his idea for a twice-weekly soap to Channel 4 Chief Executive Jeremy Isaacs in Channel 4's pre-natal stage.

Real Estate for a Realistic Series
The show Redmond pitched was called *Meadowcroft* and was set on a private housing estate, not a council estate. While these aspects would alter in production, the most startling angle of the new programme didn't change: it would be shot in real houses, not in TV studios. Filmed on video tape for added realism, and featuring a broader spectrum of people than the established 'upper-class' soaps, this programme would pioneer new realms of reality.

Knowing how an early evening soap would draw viewers into the crucial evening slot, Isaacs took the bait. His decision brought into being one of Channel 4's most popular series, *Brookside*, which, incidentally, has brought some £17 million to the Liverpool economy.

Six houses on a Liverpool housing estate were chosen as the series' main locations, from purchased property today worth around a quarter of a million pounds. Each of these houses was adapted for outside filming, a process that would turn a normal homeowner's hair silver overnight: walls were knocked down and entire rooms dismantled to make room for lighting, camera set-ups, etc. The largest house went to the Grants, the lead characters on the close, and is worth £40,000. Harry Cross's home is worth £25,000. Other houses on the property became the administration buildings, technical blocks and staff canteen.

Despite this revolutionary, documentary-style approach to sets, the traditional penchant for phony backgrounds isn't so easily dismissed. Bogus British Telecom

boxes were installed for outside filming, and a fake post-box was built. This serves the same function as the pub in *Coronation Street*, allowing the characters to meet outdoors – though it is certainly perverse to think that a post-box will do for a pub! The construction crew were so adept that one member of the cast allegedly posted mail, including cheques, in the box for weeks, and couldn't understand why his bank manager kept sending him rude letters.

Incidentally, that cast member wasn't the only person to be taken in by the enhanced reality on *Brookside*. When Heather's old house went up for sale in the series, a prospective buyer turned up on the close the day after the episode was aired.

A Story As Real As Life
The Grant family are the first to move into the Close from the local council estate. Bobby and Sheila's youngest son, Damon, loves football and hates school. The middle child, Karen, has high ambitions while Barry, the oldest, is the black sheep, always on the wrong side of the law. Sheila works part-time in a local bakery. Bobby holds a position as shop steward at the Fairbanks engineering firm.

Ricky Tomlinson (Bobby Grant) and Sue Johnston (Sheila Grant) who play husband and wife

Soon after the series begins, Bobby and his mates Matty and Jonah set up an action committee to stop the factory from closing. In response, Sheila and the other wives of factory workers form a coalition which gets recognition for the workers' plight on television. But this is not enough: the factory closes. On the dole and not enjoying it, Bobby, Matty and Sheila form a tradesman's agency, but the DHSS finds out.

Things look up when Bobby is elected district secretary of his union and given a new car. Working again, he takes Sheila to Benidorm and she reveals that she is pregnant. Her Catholic sensibilities are shocked when she finds birth-control pills in Karen's room. Karen, however, is still a virgin, even though she has weathered an unsuccessful rape attempt by one boyfriend. Another boyfriend, Andrew, endangers Sheila's unborn child when he knocks her over during the late part of her pregnancy, but no damage is done. Damon spends his time winding everyone up and dossing about.

Barry and his friend Terry have become involved with local villain Tommy

Simon O'Brien, who played Damon Grant, with his real-life brother Nick.

McArdle. Barry and his girlfriend Celia set up a tool-hire business that ends when Barry and Terry are first threatened and then beaten up by McArdle.

Sheila gives birth to Claire in 1985, at home because Bobby hasn't allowed enough time to get her to a hospital. In her subsequent depression she becomes convinced that Bobby is sneaking around with Janet Hanson. To ease matters, Bobby privately has a vasectomy. Damon starts a Youth Training Scheme as a decorator. Karen goes to university while Sheila and Matty take further education classes. Barry comes home for Christmas and is followed by a junkie girlfriend, Jane Smith. Karen loses her virginity. Damon finishes his YTS course but no job is forthcoming.

Matty takes a shine to Mo Francis, a classmate and Sheila wants to tell his wife Teresa. But Alan, a teacher, has got eyes for Sheila. When Sheila is raped emerging from a taxi, evidence points to Matty. He's arrested and Teresa kills herself, believing the allegation is true. Later, however, the police release Matty and arrest taxi driver Arthur Dutton. Karen and Barry help Sheila cope with her post-rape anxiety, but she feels that to be cleansed she must see the Pope in Rome.

After taking a job at a pub to earn the money, she persuades Bobby to go with her and the experience heals their marriage.

Harry and Edna Cross have bought the bungalow from Alan Partridge. When Harry has a slight heart attack his wife worries that the stairs will prove too much for him. Their friend Ralph comes to stay when his wife dies. The two go gambling together at a bookie's, but when Edna wins the bookie refuses to pay. Harry reports him to the gaming board but crime boss Tommy McArdle owns the shop and has Edna attacked. She has a stroke and dies in 1985. Ralph stays on with Harry and later consoles him when Harry's premature grandchild, Harriet, dies.

Leasing from the Crosses were 'three nurses' – actually two nurses, Kate and Sandra, and Pat Hancock, the hospital porter. Pat's bright ideas include a kissogram service and a van-hire which he runs with Terry. Terror enters the trio's life, in the form of John Clarke, a man Kate befriends. Clarke's mother died on Kate's ward and he blames all nurses for her death. When he holds Kate, Pat and Sandra hostage, Kate receives a fatal wound and Clarke kills himself.

Pat and Sandra become lovers but grow apart when Sandra moves to Scotland with a doctor. Pat joins a pop group, leaving Terry to run the van-hire.

Paul Collins had been made redundant when he moved into the Close. Lucy, his eldest daughter, was a problem, hating the neighbourhood. She is packed off to stay with friends in France. Later, the Collins's bright son Gordon steals money from his parents and runs off to France after a gay affair with a school chum, Chris Duncan. Annabelle, Paul's wife, sets up her own catering business and Paul gets offered a job at his old firm, only to be made redundant again a year later.

Lucy Collins returns and carries on her affair with James, a married man she met in France. She breaks down when he refuses to divorce his wife, and runs off with Barry Grant, who is off to France to sell videos. Paul Collins gets arrested in a 'Kids vs Cars' demonstration and a few months later Annabella becomes a magistrate. Gordon returns and takes up again with Chris Duncan. Annabelle's mother Mona comes to stay and drives everyone mad except Gordon, who likes her. She hurts herself falling down a hole in the road.

Certainly better off at the start than the Collinses, Heather and Roger Huntingdon are very career-minded when they arrive at the Close. She's an accountant and he's a solicitor. When he has an affair with a client, Heather finally catches on and throws him out. Single again, she herself meets a client, Tom Curzon, and they plan to marry. She later ditches him for being too domineering, and takes up with Nick Black.

Nick's a troubled bloke: he has three kids, a lesbian ex-wife and a strange friend Charlie. Nick is hooked on heroin. When he dies of an overdose, Heather leaves the Close and sells her house to Jonathan Gordon Davies and his fiancée Laura Wright, who marry in the summer of 1987. Laura has an accident and in 1988 is classed brain dead by the doctors.

Neither Gavin nor Petra Taylor has long to live after they move into the Close. When Gavin dies of a brain haemorrhage, Petra's sister Marie Jackson moves in with her. Petra soon miscarries Gavin's unborn child and has an affair with Barry Grant before running away. Marie moves in with her husband, fireman George Jackson, and his twin sons. In 1984, Petra is found dead in North Wales – a suicide. Her house goes to Marie.

George innocently describes a warehouse layout to one of McArdle's men and is arrested when McArdle's men rob it. Though he saves a child from drowning, he stands trial and Marie sets up the 'Free George Jackson' campaign. It's all in vain as George is sentenced to eighteen months in Leeds prison. Marie moves to Leeds to be near him. Terry and Michelle, Marie and Petra's sister, live in Marie's house, but Terry finds Michelle in bed with her dance teacher and moves in with Pat and Sandra.

The Corkhills' arrival soon shocks the area as it is learned that young Tracy has had sex with her teacher on a school trip. Billy Corkhill loses his job for hitting the teacher and is left on the dole. Rod Corkhill joins the police force and Billy eventually finds a job, but after an argument with his boss he gets the sack, works in the south for a while, and returns. Doreen almost sleeps with her boss the dentist for extra money, but she loves Billy too much. Billy asks his brother Jimmy to rob their house so Billy can claim the insurance money. Billy is involved in a violent robbery as the Corkhill and Collins houses are burgled. Doreen leaves Billy.

Violence and Relevance: Breaking Soap's Taboos

Brookside's most important contribution to kitchen sink drama was to add a soupçon of meaty topics the older shows had shied away from. Besides the usual smattering of affairs, tiffs, betrayals and more affairs, *Brookside* pushed soaps into the sometimes sordid world of the tabloids with stories about rape, mugging, homosexuality, drugs, suicide and child sex.

Accountant Heather Haversham, played by Amanda Burton, was a tremendously popular character who began her life in standard soap style: she and her husband, solicitor Roger Huntington (actor Rob Spendlove), spent much of their time in bed.

The tight filming conditions meant the sound engineer would crawl under the duvet with the actors, and screwy scheduling meant Amanda and Rob would be filmed eating evening meals at 8.30 a.m.

Roger's marital infidelity brought floods of warnings for the innocent Heather, but that was bliss compared to the twists of 1986, when Heather met and married heroin addict Nick Black. The plot, a stern caveat to the burgeoning numbers of heroin users in the UK, ended with Nick's overdose and death. As Amanda left the show, Heather walked from the plot alive as a concession to her legions of admirers. Incidentally, Alan Rothwell, who played Nick, was in the first episode of *Coronation Street* in 1960 as Ken Barlow's younger brother David, a role he played for eight years.

An outstanding exercise in television's power, the rape of Sheila Grant was nearly as hellish for actress Sue Johnston as for her victimised character. Sue had bravely agreed to the producers' plans for the rape despite vivid memories of a personal attack she had endured some fifteen years earlier.

For her acting ordeal, Sue was liberally daubed with mud before being dragged through the woods by her assailant. Make-up artists daubed more and more mud on Sue as the scene went through numerous gruelling retakes. The finished rape scenes spurred nightmares for the actress, and had to be carefully cut to temper their shattering impact, further cuts being made for the Saturday omnibus edition. After filming was completed, Sue wore home the phony cuts and bruises from her 'attack', to prove to her seven-year-old son that the injuries he saw on TV weren't real.

This, in fact, was the second TV trauma Sue underwent after experiencing the real thing. Sheila suffered post-natal depression after a pregnancy in her forties, and Sue had a baby in her late thirties.

Realistic mayhem hit its soap opera high in the summer of 1985 with the siege at Number 7 Brookside Close, which lured an extra million viewers to the regular seven million. Blaming nurses for his mother's death, mental patient John Clarke held Sandra, Kate and Pat hostage in a nerve-jangling confrontation that was almost as terrifying behind the scenes. Actress Sheila Grier (Sandra) claims she and her co-stars were drained physically and emotionally by the twelve-hour-straight shooting day, a savage schedule imposed to sustain the live-wire tension and desperation required for the situation.

In one scene, actor Robert Pugh (playing Clarke) roughly hauled Sandra on to the settee and poked a gun into her temple. The complex and violent action for this scene required ten takes, after which the blonde bombshell Sheila had been manhandled and prodded into a real state of nervous anxiety, shaking with terror. Clarke's suicide brought the siege to its fatal finale, but not before his lethal shot took Kate (Sharon Rosita) from the *Brookside* roll-call.

Something about sexy Sheila Grier just brings out the Raymond Chandler in the writers. Another episode called for Pat Hancock, enraged at Sandra's latest fling, to try out his right hook on Sandra's chin. The misjudged blow from actor David Easter was hard and real enough to knock Sheila to the floor.

Relevance and realism don't have to mean buffeting women about, as the series proved with a very sensitive story about a teacher/pupil relationship. Gone were the histrionics normally marking such entanglements on TV, as teacher Peter Montague (Mark Draper) and schoolgirl Tracy Corkhill (Justine Kerrigan) had an affair that garnered accolades from critics and viewers. Justine was, in fact, studying for O levels during filming, and the *Brookside* crew made sure to shoot her scenes outside school hours.

Other ground-breaking story-lines have seen Bobby and Paul Collins made redundant (spot the long-time *Brookside* character who hasn't been made redundant), Damon finding there's no job at the end of his YTS, Petra Taylor committng suicide, and spates of robberies, prison terms, faulty roads and heart failures. The series' willingness to take a chance, combined with the consistently high quality of its scripts, was instrumental in luring an audience filled with people who considered most soaps too lowbrow. *Brookside* manages to transform the standard soap elements into something more like high drama.

Backstage and on the Road

The crew for this high-quality programme is a close-knit group with little time for the characters' complex affairs. The production team are largely under thirty and work a five-day week to produce the show. Their no-nonsense approach to the series belies any myths about TV prima donnas. In fact, the production staff are known as the 601 club – the meal allowance for overtime workers is £6.01, hardly a fortune even for much smaller series.

Per diems often err on the stingy side too – for a recent shooting trip to Rome, expenses for each crew member were £4.85 per day, including meals and board. The show's producers aren't always so miserly, though: they laid out £250,000 for state-of-the-art video camera and £1 million pounds for video equipment that allow the show to achieve film quality at low cost.

And when the day-to-day drag brings the cast and crew down, there's often a little travel to sweeten the pot. On-location storylines have taken Heather and Tom to Portugal, Barry and Petra to the Isle of Man, Pat and Terry to Barbados, Billy and Doreen Corkhill to Royal Tunbridge Wells and lucky Bobby and Sheila Grant to Rome.

After her sullying rape, Sheila and Bobby took a leisurely on-screen trip to Rome. Off-screen, a crew of sixteen, Sue Johnston, Ricky Tomlinson and a plane packed with video equipment soared into a breathtaking shooting schedule: sixteen scenes, eight locations, and only three days to accomplish it all. The group raced to their first set-up in St Peter's Square as soon as the plane touched ground to shoot the all-important 'Pope scenes'.

As Sue and Ricky joined the thousands massed for the Pope's address, the crew received a nasty shock – they couldn't film in St Peter's Square. After haggling with the authorities, the crew were confined to an area 100 yards away from the Square. They rigged a special lens to film the essential shots of the Pope. His Eminence appeared for only twelve minutes, and the cameramen had to get it right the first time, as in general the Pope does not do retakes. Fortunately, they got the shot, and Sheila was restored to mental health and marital bliss.

Phil Redmond can take credit for *Brookside*'s obsession with hot topics, but their top-notch treatment depends on the twelve series writers. The producer assigns storylines to groups of four writers, who pen batches of eight episodes some five months before shooting.

Only psychics could predict what will be topical five months away, and the non-supernatural series writers have missed a few events, such as the miners' strike and the bankruptcy of the Liverpool City Council. One writer, Jimmy McGovern, would like to see a system whereby they can develop episodes on late-breaking issues of note. This would mean capitalising on the mere four-week gap between filming and transmission, and must go on record as the only time a writer has ever been recorded as asking for a nearer deadline.

Brookside People

At twenty-two, Simon O'Brien had only acted in school pantomimes and had no acting ambition. He was merely accompanying a friend to the audition, but something about the handsome youth lurking in the wings caught the casting director's eye and Simon was offered the enticing role of Damon Grant.

Simon's numerous female fans thrilled to a centrefold spread he did – not in *Playgirl*, but a more tastefully clothed one in *Jackie*. But Simon is more than just a teenybopper's delight, as proved by his success as Kav in *Stags and Hens* at the Nottingham Playhouse. Simon left the series in 1987 after being killed off, at his request, in *Damon and Debbie*.

Another star launched by the *Brookside* series is Alexandra Pigg, then a nineteen-year-old smitten with the glamour of a twice-weekly soap. Her series life came to a tragic end when her character, neurotic housewife Petra Taylor, committed suicide after the death of her husband. But Petra's demise proved a happy event for Alexandra, who went on to turn critics' heads as a quick-tongued Liverpudlian lass in the highly successful film *Letter to Brezhnev*.

When Ricky Tomlinson landed his *Brookside* role, he was having a hard time shaking

Jim Wiggins (Paul Collins) and Doreen Sloane
(Annabelle Collins).

off his rocky trade unionist past. One of the infamous Shrewsbury Two in the 1970s, Tomlinson had served a two-year stretch in prison for intimidation during a building workers' strike, and spent much of his time in solitary confinement. He worked the northern club circuit as left-wing comedian 'Hobo Rick' following his time inside, until he spotted an ad for trade unionists with Equity cards, and became the union official on *Brookside*.

Ricky, who turned down a role in Roland Joffe's film *The Mission* for the series, has strong ties with the character Bobby Grant, and runs an agency for young actors. He also wears the same clothes as Bobby, and is often believed to be in costume when spotted in public. Bobby Grant has become a working-class hero for the country – the

Socialist Worker once described him as the left's top Liverpudlian, beating out Derek Hatton.

Not everyone in the cast appreciates such strong identification with character. Although she initially said that she and Annabelle Collins had a lot in comon, Doreen Sloane has come to regret that statement: fans expect her to be fully as stuck-up as the snobbish part she plays. The series producers have drawn on Doreen's catering talents to create Annabelle's catering business, further linking the two.

Doreen came to the series as a soap veteran, having taken on four parts in *Coronation Street* and two in *Emmerdale Farm*.

(Above) *Amanda Burton (Heather Huntingdon)*.
(Right) *Ricky Tomlinson and Bill Dean*.

Her C.V. also includes the films *Chariots of Fire* and *Yanks*, television productions such as *Nearest and Dearest* and *Last of the Summer Wine*, and YTV's school programme *How We Used to Live*.

Despite the rough-and-tumble scenes inflicted upon her character Sandra, Sheila Grier has remarked '*Brookside* has taught me a lot. I've learnt to believe in myself as an actress, and to be able to immerse myself in the character I play.' Sheila left the series in 1986, and has since been in ITV's *Taggart* – where one hopes the stunt woman took Sheila's lumps for her.

Mark Burgess, who plays gay Gordon Collins, has also suffered from his realistic role. Mark remembers the grocer who refused to sell him a packet of biscuits, just because the previous evening Gordon had been seen drunkenly driving over the family dog! Mark and his wife Elizabeth met backstage at the Wimbledon Theatre and now have a daughter Romy.

Welsh Stifyn Parri plays Gordon's gay lover Christopher, and started his soap career in an all-Welsh series, *Cole*. Stifyn has begun work on a community theatre project in Rhosllannerchrugog, his home town.

Amanda Burton had been seen on TV in Granada's *My Father's House* and on a programme for BBC's *Open University*. The

An actress since the age of fourteen, Kate Fitzgerald has been a member of Liverpool's Everyman Theatre and has performed in several Shakespearean productions. Her television debut came in Willy Russell's *Daughters of Albion*, and she played Rita in the original stage production of *Educating Rita* before becoming Doreen Corkhill.

Not one but two members of *Brookside* have connections with Paul McCartney. Sue Johnston, a member of an amateur drama group after leaving school, worked for Brian Epstein, The Beatles' manager, in the heyday of the Mersey sound. She even received a personal invitation from McCartney to his twenty-first birthday in the swinging sixties.

For his part, David Easter (Pat Hancock) appeared in Paul McCartney's financial fiasco *Give My Regards to Broad Street*. He also writes songs in his spare time and has released a record, 'Lady Soul'.

The source of much backstage laughter – so much so that they have been nicknamed 'Laurel and Hardy' by the giggling cast and crew – Ray Dunbobbin and Bill Dean had peculiar histories for soap stars. Ray Dunbobbin had written scripts for *Coronation Street* and *Z Cars*, as well as for radio series. He has also appeared in both *Emmerdale Farm* and *Coronation Street*. His wife, Christine, appeared alongside Ray in September 1987 – she played Mrs Miller, a woman pretending to be a distant relative of Ralph.

Bill Dean, a former local government officer in Liverpool, had turned actor to play the lead in the BBC's *The Golden Vision*, and also appeared in such films as the raucously controversial *Scum* and *Night Watch*, starring Elizabeth Taylor and Laurence Harvey.

Twenty years on the Cunard Cruise Line in the Catherine Division was plenty for Tony Scoggo. During that long run he learned to play guitar and later worked the club scene, even playing with Ricky Tomlinson on occasion. Now known to viewers as Matty Nolan, Tony hosted 1986's Soap Aid in Liverpool with Ricky.

Some say Brian Regan has become the new heart-throb of the series as Terry Sullivan. Brian earned his Equity card as a theatre stage manager, and later furthered his

daughter of two actors, Amanda studied drama at Manchester Polytechnic School of Theatre and made her debut in *Panto*. When she announced her decision to leave the series in the 1986/7 season, the producers kept her character, Heather, alive just in case. She has since been seen on TV's *Boon* as a policewoman.

acting career in the children's soap *Murphy's Mob*.

A member of the civil service until 1950, Jim Wiggins (Paul Collins) trained as a teacher and has been a deputy head of a Liverpool school. As an actor, he has played everything from Fagin to King Lear on the stage, and he has also directed a version of Alan Ayckbourn's play *The Norman Conquests*.

Other actors on the series have various credits and connections to their names. Jason Hope (Rod Corkhill) shaved his head for the BBC Belfast production of the Irish play *Attachments*. Justine Kerrigan's grandfather Peter, also an actor, is famous for his role in *The Boys from the Blackstuff*. John McArdle (Billy Corkhill) is a former member of the East 15 Drama School and has twice appeared on *Coronation Street*. Shelagh O'Hara (Karen Grant) would love to star in a remake of a Bette Davis film in the same role as her actress heroine. Paul Usher has a band, Thrown Together, which can be seen in Liverpool clubs.

In addition to its regular cast, the series has had some famous guest stars. Astrologer

John McArdle who plays Billy Corkhill.

Russell Grant played himself on *Brookside* and is president of the Brookside Appreciation Society. Also playing herself in the series was Paula Yates, TV hostess, journalist and wife of Bob Geldof.

Awards and Acclaim

Though critics have sniped at the series for ignoring some vital issues, these complaints haven't dimmed the series' success. In 1986 it won the Royal Television Society's award for best serial, given for its realism and relevance to contemporary life. In January 1987 the *Sun*'s readers gave kudos to actors Shelagh O'Hara and Simon O'Brien, and some 20 per cent thought the siege at 7 Brookside Close was the most thrilling event in the soap year. Pop stars Boy George, Tracey Ullman, George Michael and Paul Young are among the show's avowed fans. *Brookside* has even moved into merchandising with T shirts, sweat shirts and mugs, as well as books based on scripts.

Brookside has won over liberals with its non-traditional approach to character and situations, along the way drawing fire from Mary Whitehouse, who complained to the IBA about the show's 'obscene' language. Ironically, the *Guardian* was slow to appreciate the series, and a review the day after *Brookside* opened read, 'We will not grow to love the Grants or the Collins with their microwave ovens, potted plants and foreign cars.' Initial grumblings such as these later gave way to support from left-wing quarters.

Signs of the Times

But has the series gone yuppie? This question began to plague reviewers and viewers in 1987, when Steven Pinner and Jane Cunliffe were brought on to the series as Laura and Jonathan Gordon-Davies.

Unlike the Grants, a working-class family with a shop steward husband when they entered the Close, Laura and Jonathan are lawyers, young and handsome. Many have claimed they are simply too posh for the series. Certainly their wedding, which commemorated the 500th episode in August 1987, was a yuppie extravaganza. But Redmond and company have tried to inject some relevance into even these characters'

Steven Pinner (Jonathan) and Jan Cunliffe (Laura).

lives: Laura and Jonathan had a pre-wedding AIDS test.

In spite of these complaints, actors Pinner and Cunliffe were welcomed to the show with the usual high jinks. On the set for their second week of filming, they were told to hold an on-screen kiss until the director cried 'Cut!' The obedient newcomers obeyed — and continued kissing for several minutes while the crew (who naturally were not filming) collapsed with silent laughter.

But many fear the hard-hitting show, which opened the door through which *EastEnders* would later rampage, has gone soft. In today's upwardly mobile times, ideals of the 1960s are often left behind. A writer for the series told *Time Out*, 'It's true, we are becoming more middle class, we've shifted to the right and we are no longer as polemical as we used to be.'

A dispute in 1987 with the ACTT certainly didn't help the show's union-loving image. And many members of the cast faced the end of their *Brookside* careers as the 1987 season drew to a close, including David Easter, who began work at the Playhouse, Charing Cross, on a musical with Hazel O'Connor. Kate Fitzgerald has also left, and when Karen Grant was sent to college in London, Shelagh O'Hara found herself redundant as well. Television critics began murmuring about the series' high turnover rate when producer Stuart Doughty left in November 1987 to produce *Emmerdale Farm*.

Mersey TV and *Brookside* also surprised viewers with Britain's first soap spin-off. *Damon and Debbie*, a three part mini-series screened in November 1987, showed Damon and Debbie from *Brookside* leaving Liverpool and eloping. Called a contemporary love story, this production capitalised on the appeal of its two young stars, Simon O'Brien and Gillian Kearney.

Despite a continuance of relevant storylines – AIDS pounced on the Close in 1987 – *Brookside* has begun to lean towards the middle of the road, where its viewers are presumed to be huddling. How far it will go, and how much Britain will accept this shift, remain to be seen.

Brookside

First episode credits:
Transmitted 2 November, 1982
Created and produced by Phil Redmond
A Mersey TV Production for Channel 4

Original Cast List

Character	Actor
Bobby Grant	Ricky Tomlinson
Sheila Grant	Sue Johnston
Barry Grant	Paul Usher
Damon Grant	Simon O'Brien
Karen Grant	Shelagh O'Hara
Heather Huntingdon	Amanda Burton
Roger Huntingdon	Rob Spendlove
Annabelle Collins	Doreen Sloane
Gordon Collins	Nigel Crowley
Paul Collins	Jim Wiggins
Lucy Collins	Katrin Cartlidge
Gizzmo Hawkins	Robert Smith
Ducksie Brown	Mark Birch
Matty Nolan	Tony Scoggo
Susi	Helen Murphy
Pauline	Jeanette Debbs
Priest	Peter Holmes
Grift	Gary Roberts
Jacks	Paul Stanton
Fay	Michelle Edwards
Dawn	Mary Fay

8
EastEnders –
Sex, Drugs and Unmarried Mums

From Shakespeare's Hal and Falstaff through Dickens's Artful Dodger to the Kray Brothers' Mafia, the East End has spawned many of England's most colourful legends. There's a feel to the place that informs the very words East End – simply by happening there, an event leaves the ordinary world for a surreal realm of urban magic. Sleazy, sexy, always changing and exciting, the East End is a place where rumours and myths run amok.

Such a place is the perfect venue for the shady goings-on of a soap opera. By harnessing the natural forces of the East End, *EastEnders* has made the next major stride in soap operas. *EastEnders*, like *Dallas* and *Dynasty*, is partly successful because the milieu is so well-formed, so much more captivating than the standard middle-class boudoirs. But unlike its competition, *EastEnders* also strives to be real, and so has generated more interest than any British TV series of the decade.

This series for the future began with a relic of the past: Elstree studios just outside London, offered for sale by Central TV in 1983. Elstree, home to such ATV series as *Emergency Ward 10*, was purchased by the BBC, who then asked Julia Smith and Tony Holland to develop a soap opera to occupy the empty studios. Previous BBC soap attempts included *Angels*, set in a London hospital, *Triangle*, contained on a passenger ship which cruised the North Sea, the short-lived *Tycoon* and *The Doctors*. Londoners

Smith and Holland came up with something a bit more close-to-home than medical and nautical themes: a tale of everyday life in the East End. With the BBC's approval, they developed the first two years of scripts, and producer Smith initiated a policy of script secrecy that continues today.

Set in the pretend borough of Walford, E20, the show was originally dubbed *E8* and later *E20* until the clearer *EastEnders* was adopted. Walford, incidentally, was chosen as a cross between Walthamstow and -ford boroughs such as Stratford and Ilford. Some £750,000 was spent by the BBC on construction of outside and studio sets, most of which would represent an area known as Albert Square. Top BBC designer Keith Harris had to design an Albert Square that would last (no renovation by disaster here, *à la Crossroads*).

A Century-Old Square Since 1985

Many series rely on fantasy for sets, such as *Dynasty*, while others go for a more generic look, like *Coronation Street*. But while Walford may not appear on any map, the East End has a real visual identity, and if the sets failed to reflect that, the show's credibility would go out the window. It's worth noting the pains Harris took to create the convincing *EastEnders* look.

Harris worked from the advice of writers Smith and Holland as to the characters and their likely surroundings, and used hundreds of photos of Victorian squares in Hackney

The Fowlers accepting the Oscar for BBC television programme of the year.

and Bethnal Green to get the details right. General plans were drawn up, using blueprints by Victorian architects for style. Construction crews fitted the Elstree studios with trenches for camera cables, then laid drains, built roads and pavements and began erecting the buildings of Albert Square.

On top of steel frames, they laid plywood and plaster shells. For the brickworks, casts were taken of an East End brick wall, and the mould then filled with plaster and painted. Realistic details of slates, archways, lintels and bay windows were obtained in the same way. Period doors were rescued from demolition companies renovating in the area. Sash windows, drainpipes and chimneys were built to look like the real thing.

These weren't real homes, of course, and most only had three sides. Metal platforms,

built for actors to stand on when leaning from first-floor windows, are virtually the only 'furniture' inside these constructions. But neither are they strictly decorative, for being exposed to weather, they must withstand wind and rain, and to make rooftop chases possible, the roofs are fully strengthened. Real telephone boxes and poles from British Telecom and lamp-posts from the Hertsmere Borough Council add still more authenticity.

The construction crews created more than a new Victorian square, though. Albert Square, according to the script, came into being more than a century ago. To age the sets, workers chipped the pavements, built uneven walls, cracked their careful paint-work with a special chemical and splotched the railway bridge's belly with varnish. Weeds were added to pavement cracks and around trees. No builder would be proud of the end result, but it convinces millions of viewers each week that they are watching life in a realistic East End.

The production staff paid no less attention to the interior sets for Ali's Cafe, the laundrette, the Queen Vic and the individual houses. All have working gas and water, and are fully functional. Amazingly enough, Sue and Ali of Ali's Cafe could cook you a real meal, Pauline could do your laundry at the laundrette and you could get legless at the Queen Vic, especially as the pub uses real beer for drinking scenes – fake beer looked, well, fake. (In contrast, Angie drinks herself blind on ordinary tap water, which passes for spirits on the show.)

Forays to real East End houses provided the inspiration for the furniture, curtains, crockery and other bric-à-brac in the sets. The costume department supplied a full wardrobe of work and leisure wear for each character, based on specific instructions from the show's creators. They also came up with drawers of extra clothes, marked 'Naff Handbags', 'Tacky Tracksuits', 'Tramps and Winos', etc.

Thousands of aerial photos merged into a 9 ft × 7 ft illustration for the series credits, over which would be played a hypnotically catchy tune by Simon May and Leslie Osborne. Simon May's credits include *Crossroads* singles 'Born with a Smile on My Face', 'We'll Find Our Day', and 'More Than in Love', while Leslie Osborne wrote the themes for *Buccaneers* and *Blood Money*. The pair had collaborated before on the theme for *Howard's Way* and on Marti Webb's 'Always There'. Traces of a silter and Caribbean drums, barely audible in the *EastEnders* theme, suggest the East End's multi-racial mix.

Dramatic Debut

The BBC started the *EastEnders* blitz with a press preview on 10 October 1984. Advance word from attendees labelled the series as a worthy addition to the top ranks of British soap, alongside *Coronation Street* and *Brook-*

side. When the 'new look' BBC began on 17 February 1985, Wogan's first guest was Wendy Richard, due to play Pauline in *EastEnders* the following evening.

Finally, the public got its first look on 18 February at 7 p.m. 'Dirty' Den started scheming, Angie started drinking, Albert Square buzzed with lurid energy and Britain was never the same again. By week two *EastEnders* had leapt into the top ten with more than 17 million viewers on the Tuesday and more than 14 million for Thursday.

The press lauded its no-holds-barred exploration of London's seamier side. The public adored the selection of ripe, rebellious, raunchy and real characters. Everyone loved it but the rivals. Thames TV went so far as to programme *Emmerdale Farm* directly opposite the newcomer. When the more established series took a healthy bite out of *EastEnders*' ratings, the BBC moved it to 7.30. *EastEnders* later topped the national ratings, even beating *Coronation Street*!

Behind the phenomenal success of *EastEnders* was Dennis Watts, known as 'Dirty' Den, whose turbulent marriage to Angie formed the early backbone of the series. The landlord of the Vic, Den is a philanderer nonpareil who seduced teenaged Michelle Fowler and fathered her illegitimate daughter, and divorced his long-suffering wife in the cruellest manner.

Square Stories

As the series opens, Reg Cox is found dead by Den, Arthur and Ali, who suspect murder. Pauline is pregnant in her forties, Arthur Fowler is out of work and nasty Nick Cotton, son of honest Dot, harasses Naima and Saeed, Ali and Mark Fowler. Mark goes missing but is found in Southend by the Fowlers on New Year's Eve 1986.

Angie Watts starts hitting the bottle and has a brief affair with handyman Tony Carpenter. Ali and Sue must cope with tremendous grief when their child, Hassan, dies suddenly in his crib, despite the efforts of male nurse Andy. Comforted by Andy's girlfriend Debbie, Sue seeks solace in looking after Mary's illegitimate baby,

Opposite *(left to right) Fallon, Jeff and Miles Colby of* The Colbys.

Annie. Pauline Fowler, meanwhile, gives birth to her and Arthur's son Martin.

Pete Beale's son by his first marriage, Simon, turns up and there is friction between Ian and Wicksy. Unmarried Michelle finds that she's pregnant: Andy, Ali, Lofty, Kelvin and Den are all thought to be the father! No one in Albert Square knows but Michelle and the guilty party, whom she surreptitiously meets by the river . . . Surprise! It's Den. Michelle will now pay with a child for their unacknowledged one-night-stand in the Queen Vic.

Den's lover, Jan, makes an unannounced appearance at the Vic's drag night, to everyone's shock. Angie, meeting her for the first time, attempts to drink herself out of her depression. Nick tries to blackmail Kathy after breaking into Dr Legg's office, reading Kathy's records, and discovering she was raped in her 'teens and bore a child.

Angie takes a drug overdose in the Queen Vic late at night, but Den finds her as he comes back after a night with Jan, and saves her. Mary turns to stripping to help pay for Annie's support, but this isn't enough and she finds bigger gains in prostitution. Pete's ex-wife Pat Wicks shows up to see her son Simon who, she tells Pete, is not his son!

Michelle's baby, Vicky, is born. Visiting her in the hospital, Den is shocked at the name. Lofty asks Michelle to marry him, despite the fact that she won't tell anyone who Vicky's dad is, and she accepts.

Inventing a tale that she is dying and has but six months to live, Angie gets Den to dump Jan and take her on a second honeymoon to Venice. Den meets Jan in Venice anyway. Angie tells a barman about her scheme, unaware that Den is eavesdropping. He plays along with her lie.

Colin Russell arrives in the Square and starts a relationship with Barry Clarke. Andy and Debbie go through a bad patch and Andy has a quick fling with Angie, while Debbie messes about with Roy Quick, a police sergeant. This leaves Naima in the middle as their mutual friend and negotiator – Saeed has gone home. Debbie and Andy reconcile their differences but after another

Wendy Richards (Pauline) and David Scarboro (Mark Fowler) play mother and son.

row Andy leaves the house and is killed as he tries to save a young boy from being run over.

Wedding bells will ring in September – that's the news from Michelle and Lofty. Arthur, Michelle's father, boasts about what a grand wedding it will be, which puzzles Pauline and Lou, who know how poor he is. In fact, he has stolen the Christmas Club money to pay for the affair. On the big day, Michelle dons the beautiful gown Kathy has made for her. Just before she leaves, Den pops in, gives her a gold pendant and says how much he loves her. Tormented, Michelle leaves Lofty at the altar.

A few days later, Lofty suffers an asthma attack that lands him in hospital. A guilty Michelle makes friends with him again, and they marry successfully. Arthur fakes a break-in at his house to cover up the Christmas Club money's loss, but the police are on to his scam and arrest him. He's convicted.

After months of pretend niceness, Den tells Angie he's divorcing her at Christmas 1986, and will marry Jan. Angie and their daughter Sharon move out. Arthur has a nervous breakdown while baby-sitting Martin and Vicky and wrecks the house – in the new year he is sent to a mental hospital and later serves a month in prison.

Mary loses baby Annie to her parents after they visit. Angie dries out and takes a job in the rival pub, the Dagmar, run by Willmont 'Collis' Brown. Dot Cotton shuns gay Colin and fears he may have given her AIDS through drinking glasses at the Vic. Ethel breaks her hip and moves into a hospital for old people, while Pat Wicks takes Ethel's flat and quickly becomes the Square's most hated woman. Kathy joins the Samaritans. Pat Wicks is attacked and Pete Beale takes the rap. Weeks of worry end when Pat's attacker assaults Debbie, who beats him off and identifies him as other than Pete. Debbie marries Detective Sergeant Rich and the couple leave the Square.

Eastenders first anniversary, inside the Queen Vic.

Ethel returns to the Square, feeling better, and moves in with Dot. Arthur also comes home, a changed man after his stay in the hospital and joins a Restart scheme, enjoying every minute of honest work. He also preaches optimism to Mary. Pauline takes several jobs to help pay back the money Arthur stole. Kelvin romances an older woman against his family's wishes. Sharon and Simon start dating, but Sharon remains chaste on Michelle's advice. Barry worries he may have AIDS, and he and Colin sigh with relief when the tests come back negative. Naima continues to buck her Indian family for the right to run her corner shop by herself.

Pat finally tells Pete that Simon's father is Kenny, Pete's brother - she and Kenny had an affair more than twenty years earlier. Den has an affair with Mags, but she double-crosses him by sleeping with Wicksy when Den's away importing drugs. Angie and Den call a cease-fire in their war on each other and start to become friends. 1988 comes to Albert Square with Michelle telling Pauline she is pregnant by Lofty.

Den and Angie on the Rocks

Hidden within this brief synopsis are the juicy plot-lines that have enthralled Britain and make up one-half of the nation's top ten most-watched television programmes. Of this list, number eight, with 23.55 million viewers, is a Christmas 1985 *EastEnders* that resolved Naima and Saeed's marriage problems and showed Angie finding the pub's stolen money in Sharon's bedroom. One year later on 23 December 1986, 23.9 million people tuned in to watch Albert Square's nativity play, featuring Michelle, Lofty and Vicky, making this Britain's seventh most-watched TV episode.

The three top *EastEnders* episodes, rating as numbers one, three and five in Britain's television ratings pantheon (see Appendix 1), involve the death twitches of Angie and Den's marriage, beginning in February 1986 with Angie's suicide attempt. She'd had enough of Den's affair with his lover Jan, and tried to do herself in after the Vic's closing hour. Downing a horse-choking handful of pills with her usual gallon or two of gin, Angie was found by Den, in a freak stroke of luck, and racked up 24.35 million viewers for the number five position. The controversial episode, which graphically showed Angie's method of self-destruction, was cut for the Sunday omnibus edition after viewer complaints.

Whilst convalescing under Den's care, Angie came up with a foolproof scheme to win back her romeo husband. In one of *EastEnders'* most dramatically acclaimed episodes, Angie told Den she was dying of a terminal illness and had but a few months to live. Only Angie and Den featured in this special half-hour, filmed with few retakes by a production crew who claimed to have been exhausted by the emotion generated by the two actors.

In the summer of 1986, Den took Angie on a last-fling holiday to Venice, for which the actors and crew went on location to Italy. (*EastEnders*, a runaway ratings blockbuster, had some extra money to splash around.) But Jan was also in Venice, and when Den slid off to meet her in St Mark's Square, an innocent Angie accidentally saw them in a romantic moment. Reverting to form, Angie told a barman of her 'terminal illness'

scheme, totally unaware that Den was eavesdropping.

An unexpected shower of kindness from Den throughout the autumn masked his plan to spring divorce papers on Angie. With true malevolence, he waited until Christmas, a Christmas Angie had been trumpeting as the most terrific yet. While friends and family passed out presents over a sumptuous Christmas dinner, Den handed Angie the divorce papers with a sarcastic 'Merry Christmas'. This episode, telecast early Christmas Day 1986, drew 29.55 million holiday viewers, making it the number three most-watched show.

But the number one, the all-time most-watched British programme, beating out *Live Aid* by 150,000 viewers, was the episode shown later that same Christmas Day, when Angie and Sharon walked out of the pub, scattering the news of Den's horrible deed while Pauline learned at last that Den was Vicky's father. An astonishing 30.15 million UK residents took time out from their Christmas to watch this shattering conclusion to the marriage of Den and Angie.

Top-Notch Viewing with a Message

Less compulsive but still fascinating is Michelle's saga. One comedian has wondered what's wrong with the *EastEnders* cast and has come to the conclusion that: 'They're the only people in the UK who don't know who Vicky's father is.'

The series broke new ground with its gritty presentation of a single mother raising a child, which was intended as a practical lesson for young lovers: parenthood is tough. Producer Julia Smith intended Michelle's trials to give another message too, to parents: stand by your family. Tough though Michelle has it, Mary has it worse because she's alone. Blonde-spiked Mary has turned to stripping and prostitution to support her baby. Michelle drives the message of sexual responsibility home by encouraging Sharon to avoid sex with the supplicating Wicksy until she is absolutely sure she's ready.

Though he's now supportive, Michelle has had problems with her father, who stole the Christmas Club funds to finance Lofty and Michelle's wedding. As if this weren't enough, Den showed up in Michelle's bedroom to confess his undying love, one-half hour before the ceremony. A confused Michelle faltered even as the organ played 'Here Comes the Bride', and left poor Lofty waiting. Later they were married anyway. Michelle, however, continues to receive maintenance money for Vicky on the sly from Den. Subsequently Michelle leaves Lofty on discovering she is pregnant by him.

After a prolonged nervous breakdown, which brought floods of mail for Arthur, Michelle's father, he entered a psychiatric hospital and returned, seemingly fit and happy again. One touching episode had the newly honest Arthur losing his wallet to a thief. Whilst sullenly thinking about reneging on his promises to make good, Arthur enters the Vic and is shocked as the patrons hand him a wad of money they have collected amongst themselves to compensate for his loss.

As the soap world's first permanent gay couple, Colin Russell and Barry Clarke have also drawn the spotlight. Tidy, shy Colin and beer-drinking fun fellow Barry make an odd couple, but they've also made strides towards better representation of gays on television. This hasn't always gone unchallenged: viewers launched a storm of protest after Colin kissed Barry's hand on-screen. But the public has largely grown to love this duo, and a shudder passed through the nation when Barry took an AIDS test. Fortunately, it proved negative.

The show received early acclaim for broaching another previously untouched topic, cot death. A few months into the series, Sue and Ali's baby son Hassan died in his cot. As with its gay couple and non-white families, *EastEnders*' strength is to make the commonplace into moving drama.

Credit for the series' relevance must go to Julia Smith. As co-creator and producer, she has never backed down from portraying the real concerns she wants to examine. 'I've never been frightened of controversial subjects,' she told the *Telegraph Sunday Magazine*. 'You can tackle anything, providing you do it in the right spirit.'

Allegedly, the BBC supports her to the degree that they've never tried to interfere with the plot directions, even when they surged into television's taboo areas. Not everyone agrees with Smith – Mary Whitehouse, predictably, has slandered the series' violence, bad language, portrayal of sleazy and gay characters and the overall un-Victorian tone. But Julia Smith is less interested in mollyifying her critics than in creating a powerful, believable, and ultimately moral programme.

Who's Who in the Square

Nicknamed 'Dirty' by the press for his maltreatment of Angie and for making Michelle pregnant, Den is a plum role for Leslie Grantham, and has allowed him to carve out his niche in soap opera history. Married to actress Jane Laurie of *Lytton's Diary*, Leslie shares little with his nefarious character beyond one unfortunate incident in his past.

As a young lance corporal in the army, Leslie attempted to rob a West German cab driver and accidentally shot him dead. While he denied the gun was loaded, he spent eleven years in prison for the crime. It was there that his thoughts turned to acting, after *Dr Who*'s Louise Jameson visited the prison in 1977. Upon his release, Leslie attended Webber Douglas drama college, and ironically played a bank robber in the BBC's *Knock Back*. He told Julia Smith about his prison term when the series began, and offered to leave, but Smith stood by him and supported him when the press uncovered his past.

Now studying to become a master of wine, Leslie has little fondness for the scurrilous Den. 'He's a chauvinist pig and a racist,' Leslie has stated. 'There's nothing likeable about him. I wouldn't drink in his pub.'

That's the sort of sentiment one might expect from Angie. Despite on-screen differences, there is no feud between Leslie and Anita Dobson, who plays Den's ex-victim. The two switched on the Christmas lights of London's Oxford Street in 1986, simply another public relations function for one of Britain's favourite 'couples'.

Raised in Stepney, Anita acted in everything from Shakespeare and Brecht to the

Leslie Grantham (Den) and Anita Dobson (Angie) at the Bafta Awards in 1986.

Rocky Horror Show before *EastEnders*, though she is best known as Jim Davidson's girlfriend in Thames TV's *Up the Elephant and Round the Castle*. Soap stardom has also boosted Anita's singing career. In June 1986 she recorded the *EastEnders'* theme, 'Anyone Can Fall In Love', which hit number 5. A year later she released 'Talking of Love', penned by Queen guitarist Brian May; Anita denied the two had an affair, citing her oppressive work schedule.

In 1986 she was made an honorary member of the Corpus Christi College – quite an honour for a woman best known as hard-drinking Angie. Though now a teeto-

Tom Watt (Lofty) and Susan Tully (Michelle) who play husband and wife in the series.

taller, Angie still favours the tart look, and Anita applies her own, completely overdone makeup, which is then baked on by the harsh studio lights. Despite such inconveniences and her character's bizarre appeal, Anita loves her job and is committed to it. Of her many alleged affairs, she says, 'I am not a nun, but work comes first.'

As Michelle, Susan Tully played the same guessing game about Vicky's father as the rest of the UK did. She didn't find out it was Den until hours before shooting the scene, when she finally received the top secret script. 'People used to wind down their car windows at traffic jams and ask me who the father was,' she says. 'They didn't believe me when I said I didn't know.'

Girls in trouble all over England treat Sue as an agony aunt and swamp her with letters soliciting advice. She's become a sort of spokeswoman for safe sex – despite the fact that Michelle's baby, until its birth, was nothing more than a leotard stuffed with padding. Sue would hang it up in Wardrobe after playing her pregnant scenes. Michelle is an emotionally demanding role, and moments such as the delivery can reduce Sue to floods of tears, but the actress says she leaves Michelle in the studio before driving home to her Islington flat. Other television credits include *Grange Hill* and *Our Show*.

Michelle once left Lofty Holloway at the altar, and though he's now her husband, 28 million people vividly recall the poor man being jilted. A sorrowful bloke as Lofty, actor Tom Watt is a sharp performer and budding playwright, whose first work, *A Few Words Over Lunch*, a comedy he wrote about two butlers, played the King's Head in Islington. Tom recently won acclaim as Bob Brierly, a falsely imprisoned man, in *The Ticket of Leave Man* at the Theatre Royal, Stratford East.

Though now a successful actor, Tom still drives the first car he ever owned. And why not, when it's a classic like a 1953 two-door series E Morris Minor? Tom prefers not to discuss *EastEnders*, due to the plethora of untrue rumours that pours from the tabloids, but will joke about the record he contributed to the '*EastEnders* Stars Sing' list: a cover of Dylan's 'Subterranean Homesick Blues' that limped to number 151 in the charts.

Many actors have played people whose minds are cracking, but few have had the chance to build up the character the way Bill Treacher has. Millions watched tearfully as Arthur Fowler suffered a mental breakdown and wound up in hospital; thousands of them wrote in, but many addressed their reassurances to Bill Treacher, so convincing was his performance.

'I try not to take work home with me,' Bill has said, 'but when I was playing those harrowing scenes, I once started crying in my own home. I had to explain to my wife that it wasn't me crying, it was Arthur.' Based on this harrowing experience, Bill started a service that helps the unemployed with their trauma.

Bill has played everything from a Beefeater in a beer commercial to a villain in *The Professionals*, and seeks career advice from his family in Suffolk: actress wife Kate and their children, Jamie and Sophie. Before each contract renewal on *EastEnders*, he asks them if he should take the role or if it will take him away from the family too much. Like the rest of the nation, Kate, Jamie and Sophie don't want to see Arthur Fowler disappear!

The only famous face on *EastEnders* when it debuted, Wendy Richard has a distinguished acting career that includes training at the Italia Conti Stage Academy and roles in *On the Buses*, *Dad's Army* and films such as *Gumshoe* (with Albert Finney). The television generation probably recognises her as the busty Miss Brahms from the BBC's *Are You Being Served?*

She enjoyed that series, and when approached for *EastEnders* asked astrologer Russell Grant to give her some advice. He said her career had come to a crossroads that would bring her happiness, so Wendy went for it. Besides the attendant success, the new programme brought the loss of her long blonde locks, which she'd cultivated for nineteen years, in favour of Pauline Fowler's shorter hair.

Once described as evoking a broken bottle being dragged down a cobbled street, Wendy's cockney voice has helped her character roles, and can be heard on Mike Sarne's single 'Come Outside'. The song, recorded when Wendy was nineteen, topped the charts, though Wendy never got more than

Anna Wing who plays cranky, busybody Lou Beale.

her flat studio fee of £15. Visitors to her dressing-room or home are astonished by her enormous collection of china, plastic and brass frogs.

Anna Wing, who plays cranky busybody Lou Beale, gets floods of fan mail from people who like her simply because she's an old nuisance! It's an unusual popularity for a talented and diverse actress whose appearances include the film *Billy Liar*, TV's *Sink or Swim*, *Sorry* and *The Flying Lady Pilot*, and theatre's *Skirmishes*.

Behind Anna's acting success is a Dickensian mysterious benefactor. The child of a poor East End couple, Anna nearly had to reject a place in Croydon drama school due to lack of tuition funds, until an anonymous well-wisher offered to help support her by paying into a post office account annually. With this money Anna also helped her

parents go through a rough period of her father's unemployment. Lou Beale fans everywhere can thank this benefactor, whose identity remains unknown.

Another actor who has scored with an *EastEnders* song is Nick Berry, who entered the charts with 'Every Loser Wins'. This song, combined with his soap fans and sexy looks, has made him a hit at nightclubs and discos, which fill with females for Nick's shows. At roughly £1800 a show, TV's Simon Wicks or Wicksy is considerably more in demand than colleague Willie the dog, who sometimes puts in appearances at the same clubs for around £160.

Born in Woodford, Essex, Nick has taken lead roles in TV's *Rip It Up*, *The Purple People*

Nick Berry (Wicksy) and Gillian Taylforth (Kathy Beale) leaving for a holiday in Barbados.

Eater and *A Box of Delights*, films such as *Party, Party* and *Forever Young*, and stage productions of *Oliver* and *Why Me?* His heart-throb handsomeness was nearly obliterated by a car crash some years ago, when he flew through the front window and fractured his skull. He now belts up every time.

Girls who swoon for Wicksy envy Gillian Taylforth, the lucky actress who plays Kathy Beale, his real life lover. *EastEnders* producers originally took two months to decide on Gillian for the role, wondering whether she looked old enough to play the mother of a fifteen-year-old boy. Gillian, who worked for a solicitor at the time, was thrilled when finally offered the role. She and her sisters, incidentally, were named for stars: Gillian after dancer Gillian Lynne, Kim after Novak and Deborah for Ms Kerr.

Pete Beale, Kathy's husband, provoked a startling reaction when he hit his former wife Pat Wicks: some women wrote in asking him to slap *them* around. This especially disturbed Peter Dean who plays Beale, as he deplores violence in any form. Peter follows Buddhism, having discovered it through fellow actor Oscar James (Tony Carpenter), and often chants in his dressing room.

Born in Hoxton, Peter is a true East Ender, and even rubbed shoulders with the Kray twins. He worked at a variety of odd jobs, including selling sheets in markets, where he was discovered one day, reciting a speech from *Antony and Cleopatra*, by Prunella Scales of *Fawlty Towers* fame. Encouraged by her to take drama classes, he landed parts in *General Hospital* and *Law and Order*, where he portrayed a wrongly jailed gangster. Peter warms up for *EastEnders* by recalling advice that Jean Alexander, *Coronation Street*'s Hilda Ogden, gave him when he played a Street lorry driver smitten with Deirdre: 'Always treat every script as a new play, and that way you're always fresh and vital.'

Ten years performing Indian classical dance seem a strange preliminary to an *EastEnders* career, but no one would claim Shreela Ghosh could bring more talent and conviction to her role as Naima. Shreela had also acted, and was in fact working for British Airways when the casting call for Naima intrigued her. Since playing the independent shop owner, Shreela has opened a wine bar called Cobblers in Bethnal Green with co-star Paul Medford (Kelvin). When she applied for the license, the *EastEnders*-

Gillian Taylforth (Kathy Beale) and Peter Dean (Peter Beale) who play on-screen husband and wife.

Opposite *Linda Davidson (Mary), with Nejdet Salih (Ali).*
Above *Paul Medford (Kelvin) and Shreela Ghosh (Naima) starting a charity race in Battersea Park.*

watching commission panel confused her with Naima. 'Why do you need a license?' they asked her. 'You've already got one.'

Paul Medford also helped Shreela keep her marriage to film director Jonathan Carling a secret. The cat got out of the bag when Shreela became pregnant, and took time off the show. She returned just three weeks after giving birth to her child, Shehnal. Shreela has now left the series but will be welcome to return as insiders say her part is to be kept open.

During the swinging sixties Sandy Ratcliff was a mod living in Carnaby Street with permed blue hair. She married a photographer at twenty and lived with her son William after the marriage broke up. Sandy found acting fame at only twenty-two as a schizophrenic in the film *Family Life*, for which she went five weeks without washing her hair and gnawed her fingernails into a ragged state. She worked as a model after that and as a bass player in the rock group Tropic Appetite, and was considering becoming a nurse before taking the part of Sue Osman. As Sue, Sandy's finest moments may be those grief-stricken scenes when she came to terms with her baby's cot death.

Nejdet Salih, who plays Sue's husband, cafe owner Ali, started his show business career folk dancing on tables in his father's steak house! Nejdet learnt English at a late age, having spent several formative years in Cyprus with his grandparents. He currently enjoys the off-screen company of fellow actor Linda Davidson. Ali is his first television role.

Linda Davidson, Mary in the series, studies at the Italian Conti stage school and

107

worked at a cabaret club called Wookey Hollow with Freddie Starr and Tom O'Connor. Four lines of dialogue in *Bulman* gave her the nerve to audition for *EastEnders*. The producers had slated Mary as a Liverpudlian, but Linda told them Liverpool wouldn't outcast a pregnant single woman, and that Mary should hail from Lancashire. They made the change and Linda worked hard on the role, researching prostitution when Mary turned to it. She met and fell in love with Nejdet Salih while working on *EastEnders*.

As dotty Dot Cotton, god-fearing chainsmoker, June Brown has found popularity with gay audiences. Like Dot, June is a heavy smoker and has a strong religious feeling. She is a faith healer, a talent she began when her daughter Chloe was born partially paralysed but was cured by a spiritualist clergyman. June obtains four names each week from the London Healing Centre – she never meets these people, but practises absent healing by praying for them.

Now married to actor Robert Arnold, June has lost a child and her first husband,

who committed suicide. She has performed with the RSC and her television appearances include *Now and Then*. Leslie Grantham saw her in *Minder* and suggested her to Julia Smith as a possible Dot. A member of *EastEnders*' 'older generation', she was delighted to see her age given in the *Sun* as forty-seven! Dot's roustabout son Nick, alleged murderer and blackmailer, is played by John Altman, who has had to adjust to playing one of the most hated men on television.

Fat Pat, Perishing Pat, Pat the Pest – Pam St Clement has heard them all about Pat Wicks, Simon's mum, Pete Beale's ex, and Albert Square's own Alexis wanna-be. The cruel epithets don't bother Pam, as she herself says, 'I wouldn't give Pat house room.'

A former journalist and teacher, Pam's a familiar face from 15 years of TV and film roles. She worked with Julia Smith on

EastEnders ladies: (back row l to r) Sue, Pauline, (front row l to r) Dot, Ethel, Pat and Kathy, the Queen Vic ladies' darts team.

Angels, appeared in films such as *Biggles*, *Doomwatch* and *Scrubbers*, played in the RSC's *Macbeth*, and graced the small screen in *The Onedin Line*, *Cat's Eyes*, *Emmerdale Farm*, *Minder* and many other series. Often typecast as large, brassy women, Pam was slated for a short stint on *EastEnders*, but was asked back six months after her first episodes.

Paul J. Medford was packing his stylish wardrobe to go study drama in Washington DC when the call came saying he'd got the part on *EastEnders*, as Kelvin Carpenter. This was too much to pass up for Paul, an actor of Barbadian descent who had attended the stage schools of Barbara Speake and Italia Conti for ten years and had several parts behind him. During his time on the series (Paul left in 1987), he was known for his sharp apparel. Co-star Shreela Ghosh, who is joint owner of Bethnal Green's Cobblers wine bar with Paul, says, 'Paul is the coolest dresser. I rely on him to buy all my clothes.'

For such a young actress, Letitia Dean (Sharon Watts, Den and Angie's adopted daughter), has quite a few roles behind her. She played Pepper in the West End *Annie*, Dawn (a friend of Damon Grant) in *Brookside*, Lucinda in *Grange Hill* (where she met Sue Tully), Sandy in London's *Grease*, and also appeared in *Love Story*, *Tales Out of School*, *Relative Strangers* and *The Bill*. She only just made it to *EastEnders*, suffering a collapse from gallstones on the way to rehearsals. Fortunately, her first scenes were rescheduled until after her recovery.

William Boyd plays upper crust James Willmont-Brown, also known as the proprietor of the Dagmar, Collis Brown and, as Den would have it, the owner of the 'poofs' palace'. Viewers of LWT's *Dempsey and Makepeace* may recognise him as a transvestite drug pusher from one episode, who gave Michael Brandon quite a shock when the latter pulled off his suspect's wig.

Not quite as popular as Den (if 'popular' is the right word), Adam Woodyatt still gets his share of romantic fan mail from Ian Beale fanciers. Trained at the Sylvia Young Theatre School, he played in the West End's *Oliver*, *On the Razzle* at the National Theatre, and TV's *The Barker Street Boys*. In the early days, Adam paid the rent as a butcher in Llandudno.

Anna Wing (Lou Beale) and Adam Woodyatt who plays her grandson Ian Beale in the series.

Born within the sound of Bow Bells to theatrical parents, Gretchen Franklin is both a true cockney and a natural actress. Through a half-century of performing she claims to have been in every branch of the entertainment industry but circus and grand opera! She played the original *Silly Old Moo* in the pilot of *Till Death Us Do Part* with Warren Mitchell. She was Myrtle Cavendish, wife to Wilf Harvey in *Crossroads* for a short time. These days she is vice president of the RSPCA, Richmond Branch and, despite her affection for Ethel's Willie, is a cat owner.

One of the few middle-class characters, Dr Legg and his polished accent stand out among the rougher voices in Albert Square. Actor Leonard Fenton trained as a civil engineer before enrolling in the Webber Douglas School and beginning a long acting career. He recently played Eric Gottleib in *Shine On Harvey Moon*.

Kathryn Apanowicz got the part of Magda almost by accident. She ran into Julia Smith at a party and Smith asked her to join the cast. The two women worked together on *Angels*, where Kathryn played Nurse Bucthins.

The youngest East Ender was little Annie, Mary's illegitimate daughter, played by baby Samantha Crown. With no acting experience or drama school history, Samantha gurgled along on a week-to-week contract, supervised by her mother. When Mrs Crown felt the child would become upset at the action on the set, she withdrew the baby from the series. Annie was sent to live with Mary's mother and made only photographic appearances for a while. Mrs Crown at first refused to let little Sam return, and a BBC *Open Air* programme discussing the child's treatment on the set further delayed the return of Samantha, which finally occurred in late 1987.

All the cast of *EastEnders* are under contract to the BBC, but two are owned outright! Yes, Roly and Willie have many years of BBC service in front of them. Julia Smith cares for Roly, while Willie, formerly in *Swallows and Amazons* for the Beeb, spends many off hours with Gretchen Franklin (Ethel). Gretchen would like to buy Willie, but the BBC has a long career outlined for the talented dog. They've even taken surgical steps to ensure no 'He's my baby's father!' headlines will embarrass Willie.

What Price Fame?

Being one of television's most popular series ever can sometimes create havoc. On the minor side hooligans and ardent fans took turns stealing the 'Albert Square E20' street sign from the lot until the crew switched to a plastic sign that is removed after each day's filming. More troublesome is the loss of scripts, since surprises and secret revelations are the bread and butter of *EastEnders*. Julia Smith and company map out plots six months in advance at a secret location in the Lake District. BBC staff shred hundreds of *EastEnders* script pages every week to keep plots from reaching the newspapers early. The papers get them anyway, of course, prompting rumours that the studios have a 'mole' leaking developments to the *Sun* et al. More paranoid BBC staffers believe the dailies rent flats on blocks neighbouring the outside sets, then spy with telescopes to see what's happening and take zoom-lens pictures.

Flattering it may not be, but all this interest merely points to the enormous success of the series. Shown throughout Australia and New Zealand, *EastEnders* has become the first British soap opera to invade America. The States' Public Broadcasting System network, which has aired such giants as *Monty Python's Flying Circus* and *Upstairs, Downstairs*, purchased a trial run of 130 *EastEnders* episodes in July 1987, and began televising in January 1988 with a two-hour special called *EastEnders, the Movie*. Like *Dallas* and *Dynasty*, *EastEnders* has that special magic, the ability to cross even national borders and stir hearts everywhere.

Eastenders

First episode credits:
Transmitted 19 February, 1985
Produced by Julia Smith
Created by Julia Smith and Tony Holland
A BBC Production

Original Cast List

Character	*Actor*
Pauline Fowler	Wendy Richard
Arthur Fowler	Bill Treacher
Michelle Fowler	Susan Tully
Mark Fowler	David Scarboro
Lou Beale	Anna Wing
Peter Beale	Peter Dean
Kathy Beale	Gillian Taylforth
Ian Beale	Adam Woodyatt
Naima Jeffrey	Shreela Ghosh
Saeed Jeffrey	Andrew Johnson
Angie Watts	Anita Dobson
Dennis Watts	Leslie Grantham
Sharon Watts	Letitia Dean
Lofty (George) Holloway	Tom Watt
Sue Osman	Sandy Ratcliffe
Ali Osman	Nejdet Salih
Tony Carpenter	Oscar James
Kelvin Carpenter	Paul J. Medford
Ethel Skinner	Gretchen Franklin

9
Neighbours –
Friends From Down Under

Neighbours was first shown on British TV on Monday 27 October 1986, some nineteen months after its premiere on Australia's Channel Seven network on 25 March 1985.

The concept was a winner from the start, coming from Australia's mighty Reg Grundy organisation whose other soaps *Young Doctors*, *Prisoner Cell Block H* and *Sons and Daughters* have been a success on British daytime TV. The organisation has also produced three different game shows and licensed many versions worldwide, such as 'Sale of the Century', 'Wheel of Fortune', and the latest co-production with BBC TV and Super Channel 'Going for Gold'. While on a trip to Australia, Bill Cotton, head of BBC TV, and Roger Laughton, head of BBC's daytime service, had talks with the Grundy Organisation about a co-production of *Neighbours* with the view of introducing a British family into the story-line. Instead it became a straight licensing deal. *Neighbours*, the everyday story of middle-class Australians, now enjoys a cult following of some 5 million viewers, five days a week at 1.30 p.m.; and another 1½ - 2 million or so caught up with the repeat showing at 10.05 a.m. And in January 1988 *Coronation Street Down Under*, as the press call it, was moved to 5.30 p.m. on weekdays, in addition to the regular 1.30 p.m. slot, boosting the ratings.

The Producer

The success of *Neighbours* must be attributed to its producers and in particular Grundy's

The main characters who star in Neighbours.

vice president of Drama Production, Reg Watson, a veteran of soap who worked in Britain for ATV Midlands. In 1964 he helped to launch *Crossroads*, and he produced, edited and wrote the show until 1973 when he returned to Brisbane. There he joined Grundy and created *Young Doctors*, *Prisoner Cell Block H*, *Sons and Daughters*, *Restless Years*, *Waterloo Station* and *Starting Out*. In *Neighbours* Watson adopts a down-to-earth approach involving ordinary people and families with whom viewers can identify. Despite the distance gap, the problems are

111

universal. And Watson points out shrewdly that although we only see a few 'neighbours', Ramsay Street is very long and more people can gradually be moved in. The theme tune, too, is already as recognisable as those of *Coronation Street*, *EastEnders* or *Dallas*. It was written by husband and wife song-writing team, Tony Hatch and Jackie Trent. Hatch wrote the original theme of *Crossroads*, which was used until September 1987. They are now settled in Australia, and their daughter Michelle has made a cameo appearance in *Sons and Daughters*.

The Goings-on in Ramsay Street

Max Ramsay takes pride in the fact that the street is named after his father, Jack. Max and his wife Maria have two sons, Danny and Shane, who is training to be an Olympic swimmer. Next door lives Des Clarke, whose marriage to Lorraine has fallen through at the last moment; he has a room to rent, since the house he bought is now too big, and the stripper Daphne Lawrence moves in. The Robinson family consists of Jim, his children Julie, Scott, Paul and Lucy, and his mother-in-law, Helen Daniels, a budding painter. Jim succumbs to the charms of Anna, Maria's sister. Danny and Shane have a car crash which puts paid to Shane's sporting career. Max blames Danny for the accident. When Shane recovers he falls for Daphne, but so has Des, whose mother is shattered to learn he's living with a stripper. Danny is falsely accused of mugging Mrs Brown. Helen Daniels meets charming Douglas Blake. Danny discovers that Max is not his real father but the product of a fling his mother had. This draws him closer to Max. Maria leaves Max. Max employs a young blonde, Terry, in his plumbing business. She falls for Paul and they marry. But, unknown to him and the rest of Ramsay Street, she has been involved with criminals and when he threatens to phone the police she tries to shoot him, Shane gets a job as a driver. More trouble hits the Robinsons as Helen plans to marry Douglas Blake, but he proves to be a fraud, tricking her into parting with her money. Des and Daphne, now in love, plan to marry. Max's hated sister Madge turns up to look after him and the boys. Daphne's grandfather, Harry Henderson, wins a cafe in a game of poker, and Daphne runs it when he goes off to tour the world. The wedding of Daphne and Des is all set. Shane is driving the bride to church and Max is giving her away. Mrs Clarke disapproves but gives them her blessing. Danny has accepted a gorillagram job on the day of the wedding. On the way to church, Shane and his party see someone they think is Danny, dressed as a gorilla, but it turns out to be a robber, who forces them to drive into the country, leaving Des at the church, again without a bride. Max leaves Ramsay Street. Enter his brother Tom. Max and Maria get back together in Brisbane. Des and Daphne make it to the altar at last.

Friends and Neighbours

When *Neighbours* hit British screens in 1986, Peter O'Brien, who plays Shane Ramsey, quickly emerged as the new heart-throb from Down Under. In 1983 Peter was just a farm boy in Murray Bridge, South Australia, with a Bachelor of Education degree. He had done a drama course at university, however, and tried his hand at modelling, when he was spotted by Grundy producers and signed up for Channel Nine's series *Starting Out*, which only ran seventeen of the twenty-six weeks scheduled. Later he appeared in episodes of *Special Squad*, *Prisoner Cell Block H*, *Carson's Law* and *The Henderson Kids*. Then he auditioned twice for *Neighbours*, winning the role of Shane. Peter has now left *Neighbours* to make an Australian series *Flying Doctor* and appear on the British stage, while his girlfriend Elaine Smith stays on in *Neighbours*.

Elaine Smith, who plays stripper Daphne, is a Scot's-born lass whose early years were spent in Largs, near Glasgow. She is now a graduate and member of the theatre in Education for Western Australia. In 1983 Elaine left Perth for Melbourne to become an actress, where she worked in TV ads and soaps such as *Carson's Law*, *Sons and Daughters* and eventually *Neighbours*. She too has now left the cast.

Alan Dale nearly missed out on Jim Robinson as the actor Robin Harrison had been picked for the part. But when contract negotiations broke down, John Holmes, one

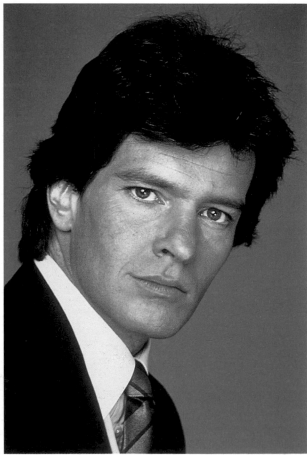

Above top *John Forsythe (Blake) of Dynasty with Joan Collins (Alexis) and Linda Evans (Krystle).*
Bottom left *Gordon Thomson who plays Adam Carrington.*
Bottom right *John James who plays Jeff Colby.*
Previous page *The cast of stars in Dynasty.*

Previous page *Marie and George Jackson who starred in* Brookside.

Below *Sandra, Pat and Kate moved into Harry Cross's house where the siege took place.*

Peter O'Brien who plays Shane Ramsay.

of the show's producers, phoned Alan, who had appeared in *Possession* and *Young Doctors*, and was working the midnight to dawn shift on Sydney radio, and asked him to join the cast.

Anne Haddy, who is Helen in *Neighbours*, is still seen in parts of the UK as Rosie Andrews in *Sons and Daughters*, although she faced the producers' axe in that soap when they found they had too many families in the show. Anne is married to actor James Condorn, who played Douglas in the show.

David Clencie, twenty-two years old, started acting at the age of fourteen, auditioning for ABC and landing a role in *Sam's*

113

Luck, a guest part in *Cop Shop*, and a regular role in ITV's daytime Australian soap *The Sullivans*. David has also been in a pop band called 'Crash Bang', playing the guitar, as Danny does in *Neighbours*.

The youngest member of the regular cast, thirteen-year-old Kylie Flinker, won her role as Lucy by crying as part of the audition, turning on the tears like a tap, and persuading the producers they didn't need to look any further. Kylie has been in TV ads for Weet-Bix and before joining *Neighbours* played in a series called *Fast Lane*.

Paul Keane, who acts the twice-jilted Des Clarke, enjoys acting whether it's soap or Shakespeare, though after two years on the show he says it's a 'psychological drain'. Paul plays drums ·for a band called 'Suitably Rough' (which also features Alan Dale, Elaine Smith and Peter O'Brien) and plays everything from Rock to Blues. Keane was

Alan Dale (Jim Robinson) and Anne Charleston (Madge Mitchell).

also a cast member of *Sons and Daughters* (he says the story-lines were unbelievable and sensational) before joining *Neighbours*.

Myra De Grout, who plays meddlesome Eileen Clarke, has had to face being poked in the ribs by angry viewers who tell her to leave poor Des alone. Myra has the best of both worlds, filming *Neighbours* in the mornings and appearing on the live stage, her first love, in the evenings.

Stefan Dennis has always played younger roles, such as young Doug in *Flying Doctors* and Paul Robinson in *Neighbours*, but in real life he's been married for seven years to Australia's 'Price is Right' hostess Roz Roy. They met while he was a trainee chef at the Gold Coast restaurant – a real life soap situation, for within six months they were living together. Both say they are too busy for children.

Ally Fowler has three soap operas to her credit: Angela Hamilton in *Sons and Daughters*, Nicola Shannin in *Possession* and now Zoe Davies in *Neighbours*. Her first scene on the show was to kiss and cuddle Peter O'Brien.

When Francis Bell was ordered to rest from his role as Max Ramsay on *Neighbours*, the producers were thrown into confusion. Within hours they found Gary Files and with only a day's notice he was playing Tom, Max's brother. Gary has lived in Canada, where he did a TV series with Frankie Howard, and in London.

When Dasha Blahova left the cast as Maria Ramsay, Max and Tom's sister Madge came to live with Danny and Shane. Madge, played by Anne Charleston, is a single mum with a teenaged daughter; and in real life Anne, who has been single for fifteen years, has a seventeen-year-old son. In 1987 she was voted Australia's top TV mum, through her role in *Neighbours*.

When he took over the role of Scott Robinson a few years ago, Jason Donovan was warned by his father, actor Terry Donovan, and his mother, TV personality Sue McIntosh, of the danger of a long-running show like *Neighbours*. Jason copes with fans remarkably well, steering clear of social involvements.

After playing interfering but much-loved Mrs Ida Jessup in *The Sullivans*, and newest TV superbitch Nellie Mangel on *Neighbours*, Vivean Gray says she prefers the latter role, which was brought into the show as a three-week run but proved so popular producers signed Vivean up on a regular basis. She had other parts in *Carson's Law* and *Prison Cell Block H*, and played a British matron in the mini-series *Anzacs* with Paul Hogan and Vincent Ball.

New *Neighbours* heart-throb Guy Pearce, who plays Mike, went on a promotional trip around Sydney and appeared on the game show 'Perfect Match', where he met girlfriend Georgie. The only problem is the phone bill as she lives in Adelaide and he lives in Sydney. With the money from *Neighbours* he has bought a house and built a gym.

Kylie Minogue, who charms viewers with her portrayal of cheeky and sometimes rebellious Charlene Mitchell, won a silver Logie award. Her sister is Danielle Minogue, a popular TV singer. Kylie's been appearing since the age of 11 on shows like *Sky Ways*, *The Sullivans* and *The Henderson Kids*.

Geoff Paine plays Clive Gibbons, who ran the gorillagram agency and having admitted to studying medicine, performed a tracheotomy on Lucy Robinson when a bee sting almost killed her. Geff is the youngest of six children and still lives at home. To this day he doesn't know why he became an actor.

Twenty-year-old Annie Jones, who plays plain Jane Harry, doesn't mind, saying she's having the time of her life in *Neighbours*. She had a role in *Sons and Daughters* as Jess Campbell, and hopes to give theatre a go one day.

Neighbours

First episode credits:
Transmitted 25 March, 1985 Australia;
  27 October, 1986 UK.
Produced by Reg Watson
Written by Reg Watson
A Reg Grundy Organisation
  Production

Original Cast List

Character	Actor
Max Ramsay	Francis Bell
Maria Ramsay	Dasha Blahova
Danny Ramsay	David Clencie
Shane Ramsay	Peter O'Brien
Jim Robinson	Alan Dale
Julie Robinson	Vikki Blanche
Scott Robinson	Darius Perkins
Paul Robinson	Stefan Dennis
Lucy Robinson	Kylie Flinker
Helen Daniels	Anne Haddy
Des Clarke	Paul Keane
Daphne Lawrence	Elaine Smith
Lorrane Kingham	Antoinette Byron
Kim Taylor	Jenny Young
Marcia Taylor	Maureen Edwards
Neil Taylor	Bruce Kerr
Mrs Armitage	Marion Heathfield

10
The Men and Women of Soap

This chapter takes a photographic survey of some of soaps' finest and most popular actors and actresses. How do the British rate in comparison with their counterparts across the Atlantic? Can they compete in the glamour stakes? And if not, what is the secret of their appeal?

Pin-ups and Pin-stripes

Certainly there's no comparison between the wardrobes of British male soap stars and their American equivalents. On American series, everything is polished to a high sheen, and that includes the clothes. British soap stars just don't get a chance to show off much sartorial splendour: Nick Berry (Simon Wicks) wears clothes from Marks and Spencer and Top Man. True, Johnny Briggs (Mike Baldwin) of *Coronation Street* does get to wear Burton's best suits, as does William Roache, but Tom Watt (Lofty) gets his *EastEnders* clothes from jumble sales and Oxfam shops.

The same discrepancy holds true in the general looks category. American soap actors are often chosen for their looks first: you won't see a spot on a *Dynasty* extra's face, whereas on most British soaps, who cares?

But in terms of acting quality and general appeal, the British are every bit as good. Watching the various series does make you wonder – how would the characters on British soaps translate into their big-budget US counterparts?

(Above) Wicksy. (Below) Mike Baldwin.

Michael Nader who plays (Dex Dexter).

Clive Hornby who plays Jack Sugden.

Maxwell Caulfield who plays Miles Colby.

Steve Kanaly who plays Ray Krebbs in Dallas.

It would surely be a big step up for most of them. Den Watts could easily take J.R. Ewing's place, for example, and might even think up a few tricks J.R. missed. Wicksy could handily fill Jeff Colby's expensive shoes, perhaps with Arthur Fowler, the ne'er-do-well never again, as big busi- nessman Jason Colby. With everyone else fleeing the Vic, Lofty Holloway could always swap places with Steven Carrington, and for a noble, wise replacement for Blake Carrington, how about Ken Barlow? Now there would be a British invasion worth talking about!

117

Grit Versus Glitter

The women of soap opera encourage female identification and wish-fulfilment, not to mention male admiration, and in so doing keep the soaps alive. Many films and even television series feature predominantly male casts, but in the soaps, one Alexis is worth a dozen handsome men.

Though few may see a striking similarity between shows such as *Dallas* and *Dynasty* and our own down-to-earth series, the types of characters on American and British soaps are nearly identical. Take Sue Ellen Ewing of *Dallas* and Angie Watts of *EastEnders*: both love fancy clothes (though not the same style, perhaps), both have two-timing rogue husbands (an ex in Angie's case) and both like a drink, or better, a bottle or two. Similarly, Miss Ellie and Lou Beale represent the motherly instinct exuding common sense and trying to hold their respective families together.

Bet Gilroy from *Coronation Street* would applaud an Alexis, and the two would probably get on quite well . . . so long as neither man nor money came between them. Pauline Fowler would jump at the chance to trade places (and houses, and husbands) with Krystle Carrington, though Krystle might find her tastes a bit hard to support in Albert Square. If Michelle took Fallon Colby's place, *voilà*! No more money worries.

Perhaps it's just as well the characters never see how the other half lives. Mavis Riley might well pine away waiting for the day she could live like Francesca Colby. Hilda Ogden might get sick of the Rovers if she saw a chance to clean the Carrington mansion – especially wearing Krystle's best! And Pat Wicks might start comparing herself to *Dynasty*'s Dominique and Alexis . . . if only Pat could manage to fit into those frocks!

Despite the lack of glamour on the British soaps, they have still produced many sex symbols. *Coronation Street* has actually come up with two: Julie Goodyear, as Bet Lynch/Gilroy, and Pat Phoenix, the Street's Elsie Tanner. Despite the regal respect accorded Noele Gordon (Meg), neither *Crossroads* nor *Emmerdale Farm* has ever spawned a true *femme fatale*. But *Brookside*'s Amanda Burton sent many a male heart racing as Heather,

118

Dynasty's *Alexis, alias Joan Collins.*

June Brown who plays Dot Cotton.

Diahann Carroll (Dominique in Dynasty*).*

Jane Rossington (Jill Chance in Crossroads*).*

Joan van Ark (Val Ewing in Knots Landing*).*

Liz Dawn who plays Vera Duckworth.

and Angie Watts of *EastEnders* is virtually a down-market Alexis Colby, though far more believable.

Nearly all the female stars of the American soaps are sex symbols of some status, but that's not surprising: many of the actresses were chosen largely for face appeal, and their pampered characters are often interesting only for their wardrobes. But it should be noted that British Joan Collins has outdone them all. Alexis has proved that a woman can be as deviously fascinating as any man, while Joan herself shows all women that there is life, love and beauty after fifty.

11
The Clothes of Soap

If the soaps are anything to go by, people in Britain and America have very different ideas of dress, not to mention vastly different amounts of money to spend on it. Can you imagine Mavis Riley of *Coronation Street* in one of Krystle Carrington's ball gowns? How about Lou Beale of *EastEnders* strolling into the Vic in one of Sue Ellen's outfits? Even 'Dirty' Den at his most dapper would seem a bit of rough next to Blake and Alexis.

The fact is that American soap operas cater largely as fantasy – the stars dress the way we might if we had the money (and, in many cases, the appalling lack of taste). Much less money is spent clothing the British soap casts, most of whom, after all, are supposed to look like regular folks.

Much of the clothing for British soaps is bought off the peg at large chain stores such as Marks and Spencer, and some outfits are even purchased by the stars themselves, or come from their own wardrobes. *Crossroads* was infamous in the 1960s and 1970s for making its cast wear their own clothes, although some actors found this much more comfortable anyway.

Not so Zeth Gladstone, a perfectly sensible dresser who found herself playing motel hairdresser Vera Downsend, a somewhat tarty woman with a flair for flash. Zeth had to lay out for mini-skirts and mod, daring clothes she would never have worn herself in a million years!

Crossroads' thriftiness began to end when Meg Richardson married Hugh Mortimer in 1975 and ATV decided to splurge on the wedding. Location filming was a big event for the series, so when Queen Meg walked down the aisle at St Philip's Cathedral in Birmingham no expense was spared. A designer from Brecknell of Birmingham created Meg's pale, mint-green gown. By the time Meg's daughter Jill married Adam Chance in 1983 and wore a dress from the Isobel department of Rachams in Birmingham, the cast were regularly smartened up in clothes bought by the wardrobe department, a requisite of the show's brighter image.

While less stingy than *Crossroads*, *Coronation Street* still depends on fashion tips that even the extras in *Dallas* and *Dynasty* wouldn't wear. Still, there's something so heartwarming about Hilda Ogden's flower-patterned pinafores, the type one can imagine one's grandmother wearing. They are now so out-of-date that members of Granada's wardrobe department spend hours tracking them down in market stalls, and the going price for these numbers averages around £3.

If that seems cheap, consider the miniscule outlay needed for Ena Sharples's old 'signature': the hair net, a few pence at finer chemists everywhere; even there, though, someone had to buy the things. Bet Lynch gets most of her earrings free in the post from fans. She's now amassed such a collection that to wear them all she would have to don a different pair every episode for the

Designer Nolan Miller dressed Dynasty's *stars.*

'80s'. Indeed, realising that its fashions were making copycat clothes into best-sellers nationwide, the shrewd *Dynasty* producers allowed the show's name to be sewn, stapled and glued on to a host of spin-off products, probably the most expensive tie-in line in television history.

At £10 or so a bottle, 'Forever Krystle' and 'Carrington' perfumes can be purchased in most chain stores, while slightly more up-market establishments stock the Alexis dress or Krystle nightie. One of the cheaper items is a wool suit from the *Dynasty* collection, a snip at £300 from Selfridges or Harrods. Of course, the true fan turns his or her nose up at such rubbish and immediately springs for the *Dynasty* collection furs, available in the UK

next thirty-five years! Sadly, we will probably never see them all, as Bet the landlady has toned down the cheap accessories and gone for a more glamorous look. But it's a sure bet Lynch will make a few generous fans happy by wearing their offerings in the coming years.

It's also a safe conclusion that none of Alexis's fashions arrived via post from secret admirers. In its bid to out-ritz *Dallas*, which used store-bought clothes from the finest stores in Los Angeles and Dallas, *Dynasty*'s creators hired designer Nolan Miller to dress its stars.

Miller, who also designed for *Charlie's Angels*, *Love Boat*, *Hotel* and other series, moulded the shoulder pad look for *Dynasty*'s 1982/3 season, sparking a trend that David Bowie has called the 'flared trousers of the

Designer William Travilla dressed Dallas's *stars.*

121

from Edelson furs. A Krystle-style wrap costs around £300, but pales beside the full-length Alexis-style fur coat at £14,500. For that price you can pick up the entire cast wardrobe on *EastEnders* and still buy a few rounds at the Vic on Saturday night. (Incidentally, they're called Krystle-style and Alexis-style because, of course, stars Linda Evans and Joan Collins have never been near the garments themselves. Buying the originals would require one's own personal fortune – even though, due to the show's luxurious standards, no garment has been worn for more than one episode.)

Realising that their names alone could move this merchandise, *Dynasty* stars Joan Collins and Stephanie Beacham have launched products on their own. Joan describes her lingerie line as for 'the average woman who wants to look sensual'. Made from easy-to-wear fabrics, the Joan Collins Lingerie Collection is available in many US department stores. Items range from $8 to $35. Buyers are enticed by photos of Joan modelling her garments and looking not at all average but certainly sensual. Meanwhile, Stephanie Beacham lent her face to the opening campaign for 'Kimberley' perfume. At £8,000 per ounce, it's hailed as the most expensive in the world.

Closing the Fashion Gap

To hit back at *Dynasty*, *Dallas* signed on William Travilla, most famous for the windblown white dress Marilyn Monroe wears in *The Seven Year Itch*. Travilla's touch is often wasted in the close-ups that dominate much *Dallas* action, but his chance to show off came when Sue Ellen emerged from her dry spell at the sanatorium in 1986. For her rejuvenated entrance at the Oil Baron's Ball, she wore a stunning, low-cut,

Larry Hagman and Barbara Carrera from Dallas *in clothes by Travilla.*

A Dynasty *wedding.*

A Colbys *wedding.*

off-the-shoulder black dress, sparkling with what were supposed to be diamonds. Travilla has since shown his hand in Angelica Nero's clothes, modelled by beautiful Barbara Carrera, and in the Travilla-inspired Southfork collection of dresses, available in the shops for around $200 each.

Mail-order firm Littlewoods had such success with the Travilla line that they asked the designer to produce a further collection. The campaign features such soap sirens as Stephanie Beacham, Tracy Scoggins, Heather Locklear, Catherine Oxenberg and Deborah Shelton.

And if you can smell like a Carrington, shouldn't you be able to smell like a Ewing? You can, if you live in the US, by dabbing a little of 'The Southfork Woman' or 'The Southfork Man' behind each ear. Of course, which particular man or woman's scent you get is up to the imagination. It may be J.R.s!

The designer look has also spread to the spin-offs. Nolan Miller enlivened *The Colbys* with gowns for British actresses Stephanie Beacham and Emma Samms (Sable and Fallon), though there is not yet a Colbys' collection. Nor are their collections based on any British soaps – but it is intriguing to wonder what would happen if such a craze did catch. Would Hilda Ogden bring the pinafore back in style? Would Dirty Den clones clutter the fashionable soirées in Mayfair? And how much would you pay for a genuine designer Benny-style hat?

12
Gone But Not Forgotten

Noele Gordon who played Meg Richardson.

Soap opera characters disappear for much the same reasons as do real people – they die, they move away, they retire. For many viewers, the absence of a favourite soap personality is barely tempered by the knowledge that the character isn't real. Real grief often follows when characters die in a series, even if the audience knows they have been 'written out' because the actor is leaving.

Real Losses

The saddest cases are those when the actor has died. Few such losses have been as great as when Pat Phoenix, who played Elsie Tanner on *Coronation Street*, passed away.

Despite her long career on the show, she wasn't thrilled with the part at first. Pat had struggled for years to lose her northern accent, and was doing quite well as an interviewer on Granada's *People and Places* when her agent asked her to reinstate the accent for a part in *Florizel Street*, the original title for *Coronation Street*. There she had to deliver lines like "Eech, you're about ready for the knackers' yard, Elsie!', but found compensation in being called the sexiest woman on television.

Her career on the Street took some twists and turns as she married co-actor Alan Browning (who played Alan Howard), left the series with him in 1973 and returned in 1976, her marriage over on-screen and off. When Pat, past sixty, decided to leave the series for good in 1984, Elsie Tanner took a long one-way trip to Portugal.

Pat's TV career continued – she worked for Tyne Tees TV as an interviewer, TV AM and on her own Central TV sitcom as a seaside landlady in *Constant Hot Water*. After a long fight, Pat succumbed to cancer in September 1986; she left in true Elsie style, with a jazzy New Orleans-style funeral that included many *Coronation Street* colleagues.

A founding member of ATV and the first woman to interview a Prime Minister (Harold Macmillan) on the station, Noele Gordon was a successful actress long before she graced the *Crossroads* set as Meg. Starting in 1947, she starred (as Meg!) in a successful West End production of *Brigadoon* that ran for 1,000 performances, and was even presented to King George VI and his Queen in November 1949 at a Royal Variety Performance.

After a stint in America, where she learned about TV production at New York University, she returned to England to join ATV as an adviser on women's programming. Also at ATV were her agent Lew Grade and her lover Val Parnell. Noele launched ATV in the

Coronation Street *after 18 years, with only five remaining members of the original cast.*

Midlands and presented some ten programmes a week, including *Tea with Noele Gordon*. Reg Watson met her on *Lunch Box* and chose her to be one of *Crossroads'* original cast.

Her character, Meg Richardson, owner of the Crossroads motel, was the linchpin of the series, and provided many of its highlights. Meg's wedding, a high point for the show, drew some 16 million viewers. Thus, it came as a shock when Noele was sacked in 1981, after seventeen years and 3,000 episodes. Amidst the ensuing blaze of publicity, the real reason for her abrupt dismissal remained unknown. Promoting her record 'Goodbye' on Russell Harty's programme the same night Meg left for Australia on the QE2, Noele's composure shattered and Harty had to soothe her tears.

After two years in New York, Meg made a return appearance to the show in 1983,

125

when she rendezvoused with the honey-mooning Jill in Venice. But there were no further appearances, as by this time Noele's stage career had kicked into high gear again in shows such as *Gypsy*, *Call Me Madam* and *No No Nanette*. New producer Phil Bowman was preparing Meg's return to *Crossroads*, but it never took place – after two operations, Noele died of cancer in Nuffield Hospital in 1984.

Roger Tonge's career was particularly poignant. From an £8-a-week clerical worker, he went on to GPO amateur theatricals, drama school and, by accident, his first professional acting job at the age of seventeen – as Sandy Richardson on *Crossroads*. Roger was applying for a part when a cleaning lady, thinking he had been called to audition, sent him into a production meeting by mistake. The producers liked him, and narrowed the possible Sandys down to Tonge and one other actor, then asked the two to react to their pet dog being run over. Roger improvised a moving and creative performance that won him the role.

As Sandy, the victim of a car accident, Roger learned to play scenes from a wheelchair; in later years he needed one himself. Roger suffered from an incurable disease, which took his life in 1981 at the age of thirty-four. At the family's request, Roger's death was never mentioned in the series. Strangely, neither was Sandy's – the character, with classic *Crossroads* confusion, simply went on holiday, and a year later was casually referred to as deceased.

A wartime performer who entertained the troops in World War II through broadcasting, Violet Carson became famous as Aunt Vi on the *Children's Hour* and as a hostess on the radio quiz *Have a Go*. When casting directors at *Coronation Street* struggled with the juicy role of Ena Sharples, Tony Warren saved the role by remembering the sharp-tongued woman Violet, with whom he'd had a run-in on the *Children's Hour* when he was young.

Violet, unimpressed with the part, took it for the money. Her original five-week contract drew her into a role she would play for twenty years. Like her character, Violet spoke honestly and humorously and was not to be bested.

One tale from the early 1960s shows how she made history as the Street's first *real* scene-stopper. When Count Basie's band was recording one day in the studio next door, their music could clearly be heard in the *Coronation Street* studio. Cast and crew continued stoically while Basie's band grew louder and louder. Violet, aware that producers forbid retakes, finally turned her eyes skyward and mouthed, 'I can't take any more!' – in the middle of her close-up. From the gallery was heard, for the first time ever, 'Stop take'.

Violet's ill health caused Ena to leave the show in 1980. She was sent off to housekeep in St Anne's and never returned. Violet herself left the world in December 1983.

Another *Coronation Street* regular, Doris Speed was the daughter of music-hall parents, and started her stage career at age five! At BBC radio in Manchester she met Tony Warren, a fan who especially admired her performance in Noel Coward's *Hay Fever*. In 1960 he invented the role of classy landlady Annie Walker for her, and asked her to read the part. Like Violet Carson, she was not moved by the part or the series at first, and she worried that the thirteen-week stint might kill her theatrical career, show business snobbery being what it is. Instead, of course, she shot to fame as the Queen of the Rovers, and stayed on until her health forced her retirement in 1984. Doris allegedly acknowledged her debt to Warren's fandom by christening her first mink coat Tony.

Emmerdale Farm grandfather Sam Pearson was played by Toke Townley, ex-film star. Toke began with the Farm's first episode and got to know the entire production crew over the years – he could often be found chatting with caterers and receptionists, and knew most YTV employees by their first names. Strangely, this friendly fellow preferred to live alone in a hotel. Toke died in his sleep in 1984.

Jim Davis played Jock Ewing, the tough father figure on *Dallas*, until his untimely death in 1980 from a brain tumour. His rugged looks and appealing drawl, not

Toke Townley (pictured with Sheila Mercier) who played Sam Pearson in Emmerdale Farm *and who died in 1984.*

126

Catherine Oxenberg who played Amanda in
Dynasty.

unlike John Wayne's, served him admirably in a host of Western movies, including *Bad Company*, *Comes a Horseman*, *El Dorado*, *Hellfire*, *The Last Command*, *Monte Walsh* and *The Outcast*. He'd fallen on harder times in the 1970s and took part in several inconsequential television films, such as *Satan's Triangle* and *Deliver Us from Evil*, before Leonard Katzman signed him up for *Dallas*. With his Western-film past, Jim was a natural for the role of Jock Ewing. When Jim died, the scriptwriters sent Jock into the jungle to look for oil, where he perished. His will put Bobby and J.R. at each other's throats.

'Suddenly Surplus'

Age and disease, of course, aren't responsible for all the missing characters. Some actors simply tire of the parts, and some characters

128

aren't good enough to keep around for long. The latter are judgement calls by the producers, which many fans feel are unfair to developing or off-beat characters.

Two to feel the axe on *Dynasty* were Pamela Bellwood and Catherine Oxenberg, both glamorous and successful actresses who won fans on the series. Pamela Bellwood's character Claudia led a typical *Dynasty* existence – she had nervous breakdowns, lost her husband and daughter and kept the Carrington men sexually active. But then Pamela became pregnant, and the scriptwriters refused to do the same for Claudia. For several episodes Claudia sat behind desks, stood behind cars, peered around doors and got more than her share of close-ups – anything to hide the Bellwood belly.

When this proved untenable in 1986, Claudia's death by fire was planned – but not well enough. When the set caught fire for Claudia's bow-out, the flames went out of control and sent Pam into the hospital. She now spends her time in her Spanish-style Hollywood home with her husband Nick and child Kerry, far from the *Dynasty* heat.

Catherine Oxenberg left the show with a different kind of fire – the lapping flames of gossip. Catherine, the daughter of Princess Elizabeth of Yugoslavia, played Amanda, the princess of an unnamed European country. It seems that Catherine's fame as Amanda went to her head, and insiders spoke of personality clashes as the young starlet, who had been compared to Grace Kelly, flounced proudly about the set. When she asked for her salary to be doubled to $14,000 per episode, *Dynasty* bosses took advantage of Catherine's refusal to show up for her pre-season physical and sacked her.

In her place came a young actress who had been doing time in hamburger joints waiting for roles: Karen Cellini, whose acting was, unfortunately, likened to Catherine's. More unfortunately, Karen and Catherine looked nothing alike, but the producers refilmed scenes from the 1985/6 season for the 1986/7 update with Karen re-enacting Catherine's part. Karen, who affected an English accent rather successfully, played the character for a year before Amanda was sent to London to live with her aunt Rosalind, a small cameo by Juliet Mills. The producers later regretted

Above right *Lofty Holloway of* EastEnders *is played by Tom Watt.*
Below *A night 'up west' for the ladies of Albert Square – Mary, Angie, Sharon and Dot.*

Above *West Ham supporters – Angie, Kathy, Den in the Queen Vic.*
Below *On screen Debbie and Andy were lovers and off screen Shirley and Ross were lovers too.*

dumping Catherine and agreed to double her pay for a return season. Miss Oxenberg gracefully refused.

Even fairly recent viewers may recall *EastEnders'* Debbie and Andy, played by Shirley Cheriton and Ross Davidson. Debbie and Andy lived together at 43 Albert Square until their love life was shattered – by the tabloid-trumpeted tale that Shirley and Ross were also lovers. Sold by Shirley's husband to the papers, these reports sparked backstage arguments and forever sullied nice-guy Andy's image. The writers responded by killing Andy in 1986 – he died a hero while saving a child from an oncoming lorry. At Shirley's request, Debbie was written out – she married a policeman who subsequently moved – but Shirley has not completely fallen from the show's grace, and may make future guest appearances.

A scandal also took Peter Adamson from the *Coronation Street* cast. Having played Len Fairclough for twenty years, Peter had suffered in the series from heavy drinking and his wife Jean's rheumatoid arthritis. In 1983, Peter, who taught swimming part-time, was accused of molesting children during lessons. Granada responded by yanking Len from the Street during Peter's trial. Though he was acquitted, Peter faced a whopping legal bill of £120,000. To pay it, he sold backstage gossip from *Coronation Street* to the press, and Granada sacked him.

Two of the favourite *Crossroads* characters vanished when producer Philip Bowman took over the series. When husband and wife management team David and Barbara Hunter were sent on a world tour – forever – even *News at 10* reported their departure! Their disappearance robbed the show of actors (and lovers) Ronald Allen and Sue Lloyd.

Ronald, who had played David from the early 1970s, had appeared in BBC's soap *Compact*, trained at RADA and spent two years at the Old Vic, where he worked with Richard Burton, John Neville and Wendy Hiller, among others. Hollywood films such as *Hellboats* made for 20th Century Fox were followed by a return to England and TV's *Armchair Theatre*.

A varied career for Sue Lloyd started with modelling, moved on to dancing and continued with acting. Her films include *The*

Peter Adamson (centre) who played Len Fairclough in Coronation Street.

Ipcress File (with Michael Caine), *Corruption* (with Peter Cushing), *Innocent Bystander* (with Stanley Baker) and the self-explanatory *The Stud* and *The Bitch* (both starring a pre-*Dynasty* Joan Collins). On television, Sue starred opposite Steve Forrest in *The Baron*, appeared in *His and Hers* and played Hannah Wild in a 1971 stage version of *The Avengers* directed by Leslie Philips. She has been seen recently in Tyne Tees's *Supergran*, but she and Ronald spend most of their time in Hollywood, where it's rumoured that Ronald is lobbying to join a US soap.

In Memoriam

It would be useless to try to detail all the characters who have left the soaps – some series seem to shake off characters every year. Further disappearances are charted in the chapters on individual series, but a final few favourites appear below:

Jack Howarth, who played Albert Tatlock in *Coronation Street*, died a natural death in 1984, as did Albert some time earlier.

Arthur Leslie portrayed Jack Walker, Annie's husband on *Coronation Street*. After his death in the 1970s, his character was killed off.

Bernard Youens provided a comic foil for Hilda Ogden as Stan Ogden on *Coronation Street* until 1984, when he died of natural causes.

And finally, there is actor Alan Rothwell, still living, whose characters tend to be rather less sturdy than he. As David Barlow, Alan was in the very first *Coronation Street*, but was written out in 1967 when his character was sent to Australia, where he died in a car crash. Alan retured to the soaps as *Brookside*'s Nicholas Black in 1985 – who, of course, overdosed on heroin in 1986. To Alan goes the special soap opera 'Farewell' award, for excellence in expiration.

On-screen and off-screen lovers, Ronnie Allen (David Hunter) and Sue Lloyd (Barbara Brady) from Crossroads.

13
Soaps –
A Royal Obsession

Despite the tabloid hoopla that turns the British Royal Family into a real-life soap opera, our royal monarchs are only human, and enjoy a bit of soap themselves. The Queen Mother, for example, is said to like the Scottish afternoon soap *Take the High Road*. She finds it relaxing, and rumours say she video-tapes it when her engagements call for her to be out.

The Queen Mother also likes *Crossroads*, an affinity she shares with her grand-daughter-in-law, the Princess of Wales. Princess Diana introduced Prince Charles to the pleasures of soap with *Dynasty* – royal observers say that Friday night mealtimes in the Highgrove house are delayed until after 9 p.m. so the Princess may enjoy Blake and company.

Princess Diana, like most of her subjects, enjoys *EastEnders* as well. A 'Dirty' Den fancier, she records episodes when not at home and watches the Sunday afternoon omnibus edition, say insiders. She has had a private visit with the cast and has even pulled a pint in the Queen Vic.

The Duchess of York, meanwhile, prefers the glamour of the American soaps such as *Dallas*, *Dynasty* and *The Colbys*. Our Queen herself is a *Coronation Street* fan, a fact kept quiet until the Queen and the Duke of Edinburgh visited Granada's studios, where the series is made. Her Majesty impressed the

Joan Collins meets Princess Diana, who is said to be a keen fan of Dynasty.

All spruced up . . . Hilda and Stan Ogden with their lodger Eddie Yeats from Coronation Street *greet Her Majesty when she made a trip to the Street to meet the actors and actresses in 1982.*

cast and the producers with her knowledge of the series. She has since invited many of the cast to Buckingham Palace.

Linda Evans, Krystle Carrington of *Dynasty*, was astonished while once in Edinburgh for a charity function, when her hotel door opened and a member of the royal house stood outside. Linda was presented with a white card embossed with the royal gold seal. It commanded her to meet the Queen at Holyrood Palace in Edinburgh – the meeting of these two extraordinary women would have been worth missing *Dynasty* for!

Our royal family aren't the only world leaders to take an interest in the soaps. Ronald Reagan regularly tunes in to *Falcon Crest*, to the annoyance of his wife Nancy: Reagan's ex-wife Jane Wyman appears on the programme. Ex-President Gerald Ford and Dr Henry Kissinger, former US Secretary of State, have gone one better by actually appearing in *Dynasty*, while Ford's son Stephen is a star of the daytime soap *The Young and the Restless*.

So that puts paid to the notion that only a certain kind of person would bother to watch these programmes. Whether you're a royal personage, a world leader or just plain Joe Bloggs, you can't beat a good soap!

14
Soap-Fan's
Quiz

EastEnders

1. How much money did Arthur take from the Christmas Club?
A. £2,000
B. £1,514
C. £2,500

2. When Michelle dyed Lofty's hair, what colour did it go?
A. Blue
B. Orange
C. Green

3. Where did Lofty propose to Michelle?
A. On a park bench in Albert Square
B. In the Queen Vic
C. In the launderette

4. What EastEnder has a neck tattoo?
A. Mary Smith
B. Nick Cotton
C. Sue Osman

5. Who found Angie unconscious when she took an overdose?
A. Simon Wicks
B. Den Watts
C. Sharon Watts

Coronation Street

1. What was the name of Elsie Tanner's first husband?
A. Steve
B. Arnold
C. Alan

2. Who rescued Ena Sharples when a train crashed over the viaduct in 1967?
A. David Barlow
B. Ken Barlow
C. Dennis Tanner

3. What is Kevin Webster's sister's name?
A. Elaine
B. Tracey
C. Debbie

4. Who died on Hilda and Stan's ruby wedding anniversary?
A. Bert Tilsley
B. Len Fairclough
C. Ernest Bishop

5. Which family was fined for not having a TV licence?
A. The Ogdens
B. The Tanners
C. The Duckworths

Crossroads

1. Which religious sect did Joanna Freeman become involved in?
A. Bright Light
B. Inner Light
C. Guiding Light

2. In which country did Kevin, Glenda and Katie Louise Banks go to live?
A. Holland
B. America
C. Canada

3. Who ran the King's Oak post office in the early days of *Crossroads*?
A. Edith Tatum
B. Amy Turtle
C. Vi Blundell

4. What was the name of the French terrorist David Hunter had an affair with?
A. Kate Hamilton
B. Simone Clavel
C. Folrance Berg

5. What was the name of the gypsy girl Benny was going to marry but who was killed on the day of the wedding?
A. Maureen Flynn
B. Alison Cotterill
C. Josie Welch

Brookside

1. Who lives at No. 5 Brookside Close?
A. The Collinses
B. The Corkhills
C. The Grants

2. In what time did Paul Collins finish the 1987 Mersey Marathon?
A. 3 hours 40 seconds
B. 5 hours 19 seconds
C. 9 hours

3. Who visited 10 Downing Street with a petition?
A. Marie Jackson
B. Sheila Grant
C. Harry Cross

4. Who held Kate, Sandra and Pat hostage?
A. Arthur Dutton
B. John Clarke
C. Tommy McArdle

5. What was the name of Barry Grant's drug addict girlfriend?
A. Jane Smith
B. Mo Francis
C. Celia Johnson

Emmerdale Farm

1. What does NY in NY Estates stand for?
A. New Yorkshire
B. North Yorkshire
C. North York

2. What is the name of the farm where Alan Turner lives and works?
A. Demdyke Farm
B. Ridge Farm
C. Home Farm

3. What was Jack Sugden's former profession?
A. A novelist
B. A shopkeeper
C. An office worker

4. What was Annie Sugden's husband's name?
A. Jack
B. Joe
C. Jacob

5. Who is the gamekeeper for NY Estates?
A. Jackie Merrick
B. Nick Bates
C. Seth Armstrong

Dallas

1. Which Southfork couple has not had their wedding on the ranch?
A. Sue Ellen and J.R.
B. Miss Ellie and Clayton
C. Pam and Bobby

2. Who did Bobby give power of attorney after being shot?
A. Donna Krebbs
B. Pam Ewing
C. Jenna Wade

3. What does J.R. Ewing's car registration number plate read?
A. Ewing 1
B. JR Ewing
C. Ewing 3

4. Who was first arrested for shooting J.R. but later released?
A. Afton Cooper
B. Sue Ellen Ewing
C. Bobby Ewing

5. What was the name of the man who gave Pam and Bobby Christopher?
A. Dave Culver
B. Peter Richards
C. Jeff Farraday

Dynasty

1. While pregnant, Krystle worked for Blake; what was her title?
A. Managing Director
B. Head of Public Relations
C. Head of Staff Relations

2. What was Adam's middle name?
A. Alexander
B. Blake
C. Tom

3. Who tricked Jeff into believing he had married her after a heavy drinking session?
A. Kirby Anders
B. Claudia Blaisdel
C. Nicole Simpson De Vilbis

4. What was Sammy Jo's maiden name?
A. Reece
B. Dean
C. Grant

5. What happened on the night Alexis married Cecil Colby?
A. Alexis left Cecil
B. Cecil was shot
C. Cecil died of a heart attack in his hospital bed

The Colbys
1. What was Jason Colby's father's name?
A. Philip
B. Andrew
C. Charles

2. Who knocked over Constance Colby Patterson?
A. Sable
B. Monica
C. Jason

3. What was Fallon's name when Miles brought her to meet the Colbys?
A. Tracey Adams
B. Fallon Colby
C. Randell Adams Colby

4. What is Miles Colby's favourite sport?
A. American football
B. Polo
C. Shooting

5. What is Jason Colby's company called?
A. Colby Towers
B. The Colby Company
C. Colby Enterprises

Knots Landing

1. What title did Gary Ewing have when working at Knots Landing Motors?
A. President
B. Vice President
C. Managing Director

2. What was the title of Val Ewing's book, said to based on the Ewings?
A. Love in Dallas
B. A Family Life
C. Capricorn Crude

3. What was Karen Fairgate MacKenzie's maiden name?
A. Cooper
B. Fairgate
C. Dobson

4. Where was Laura and Richard Avery's son Daniel born?
A. In Knots Landing General Hospital
B. In the back of Richard's car
C. In Karen's house

5. What was Chip Roberts's real name?
A. Steve Shaw
B. Bobby Jacobs
C. Tony Fenice

For answers, see page 140.

Appendix 1
The Ratings

As a barometer of a programme's popularity, ratings don't satisfy everyone, but as an indicator of general trends they are very telling. Surely it's no coincidence that eight of the all-time top ten ratings winners in Britain are soaps. *Dallas* and *Dynasty*, likewise, have provided some of America's most-watched television moments.

A look at some of the latest available figures shows how the soaps stack up against each other. The autumn and winter months are crucial, as viewing numbers are highest in September, strong through April, and then more depressed through the summer.

Soap ratings for the week ending 26 October 1986 were as follows:

Programme	Position	Viewers (in millions)
EastEnders	1	20.58
Coronation Street	4	14.80
Crossroads	10	11.70
Dallas	12	11.54
Emmerdale Farm	17	10.83
The Colbys	39	8.56
Brookside	70	6.20

Few would question *EastEnders'* ratings superiority, but we should note that figures contain the viewers of Sunday's afternoon edition, which merely repeats the week's two episodes. Many have questioned this method of reporting, though *Brookside* has been doing the same for five years.

Brookside's low score is partly due to its home on Channel 4. Chances are that the same programme on ITV or the BBC would surpass most of the other soaps, save *Coronation Street* and *EastEnders*.

Dynasty, shown on alternate weeks in rotation with *The Colbys*, does not appear.

Week ending 1 February 1987

EastEnders	1	24.07
Coronation Street	2	17.10
Crossroads	19	12.10
Emmerdale Farm	25	11.07
Dallas	31	10.67
Dynasty	46	9.08
Brookside	75	6.32

Most of the soaps have taken a small upturn in ratings since October, though the positions remain the same. Here, the advantage of *EastEnders'* Sunday repeats seems obvious, since with three transmissions instead of *Coronation Street*'s two, *EastEnders* has another half as many viewers as the *Street*. Repeat viewers are probably not keeping the show at number one, but they are exaggerating the differences between it and number two. Each Sunday *EastEnders* averages around 5 million.

Week ending 12 July 1987

EastEnders (Tu. & Sun.)	1	17.30
EastEnders (Th. & Sun.)	2	16.07
Coronation Street (Wed.)	3	13.60
Coronation Street (Mon.)	4	12.50
Crossroads (Wed.)	15	8.60
Crossroads (Tu.)	19	8.40
Crossroads (Th.)	20	8.10
Emmerdale Farm (Tu.)	21	8.10
Emmerdale Farm (Th.)	22	8.00
Dynasty	25	7.80
The Colbys	43	6.40
Brookside	67	4.80

This more detailed chart for the summer ratings shows *EastEnders* still in the lead despite the seasonal slump, and reveals that *Crossroads*, in its last months, held a steady audience with a respectable viewing figure. *Dallas* is over for the year, prompting the BBC to screen *Dynasty* and *The Colbys* in the same week. *Brookside* trails as usual.

The UK All-Time Top Ten TV Programmes

More revealing than week-to-week records is the list of Britain's all-time audience winners. Besides clearly earmarking *EastEnders* as the UK's most popular series, despite its questionable reporting method, this list puts a strange perspective on soaps' popularity. *Live Aid* and Charles and Diana's wedding are often cited as the all-time ratings winners . . . let's see how they stack up.

Programme	Position	Viewers (in millions)
EastEnders Christmas Day 1986, evening	1	30.15
Live Aid 16-hour pop show, July 1985	2	30.00
EastEnders Christmas Day 1986, teatime	3	29.55
Coronation Street Christopher Hewitt kidnapped, October 20 1962	4	26.00
EastEnders Angie's suicide bid, 28 February 1986	5	24.35
Dallas The shooting of J.R., 26 May 1980	6	24.00
EastEnders 23 December 1986	7	23.90
EastEnders Boxing Day 1985	8	23.55
Coronation Street Rovers Return fire, 18 June 1986	9	22.75
Royal Wedding of Prince Charles and Lady Diana Spencer, July 1981	10	21.00

NOTE: All ratings figures in this chapter supplied by Broadcast/AGB UK.

Appendix 2

Glossary of Television Soaps in the UK

Angels
BBC
1975-1982
Set in a large London hospital, St Angela's, this series ran twice a week but not year-round.

Brookside
Mersey TV
1982-
A twice-weekly offering, *Brookside* is set on a Liverpool Close and follows the Grants, the Collinses, and several other families and individiuals. It's hailed as Britain's most intelligent soap.

Châteauvallon
Antenne 2 Tele-Française, Tele-CIP
with Son et Lumière, Maintenon Films and RTL TV Luxembourg
1985
The rich Berg family, owners of the influential newspaper *La Dépêche*, squabble *Dynasty*-style. This 26-week, one-season soap finished when actress Chantal Nobel (playing Florence Berg) was badly hurt in a car crash.

The Colbys
ABC
1985-1987
Jeff Colby moves to Los Angeles to receive his aunt Connie's shares in Colby Enterprises, remarry Fallon, fight aunt Sable and make shocking discoveries about his family tree.

Coronation Street
Granada Television
1960-
Set in a Salford street with a pub at one end and a corner shop at the other, this is Britain's longest-running drama series.

A Country Practice
Channel 7 Australia
1981-
This Australian soap is set around a small community hospital in New South Wales and the doctors who run it, Dr Elliott and Dr Brown.

Crossroads
ATV-Central
1964-1988
Meg Richardson starts a small family-run Midlands motel, the centre of the village's social interaction. In 1981, Meg sailed off on the QE2 to start a new life, so beginning the series' downfall slide.

Dallas
CBS
1978-
The Ewings are an oil-rich family from Southfork Ranch, Dallas, Texas. Ewing Oil is run by good Bobby Ewing and bad J.R. Ewing. Their mother, Miss Ellie, struggles to keep the family together.

Dynasty
ABC
1981-
The Carringtons live in a 48-room mansion

in Denver. Blake Carrington, patriarch, runs an oil company. His ex-wife Alexis runs a rival oil company and seeks revenge on Blake for sending her away when the marriage broke up.

EastEnders
BBC
1985–
Based in London's East End, this reveals the lives of several families living in Albert Square. Sordid problems abound, with scallywag 'Dirty' Den a leading nasty man.

Emergency Ward 10
ATV
1957–1967
Britain's first hospital soap was this twice-weekly offering, detailing the excitement of the eponymous Ward 10.

Emmerdale Farm
Yorkshire Television
1972–
The Sugdens work on said farm in a small Yorkshire village. This series started as a daytime soap and is now shown in peak hours.

Falcon Crest
CBS
1981–
Set in wine-growing Napa Valley near San Francisco, the Falcon Crest Empire is wrestled for by Angela Channing Chase Groberti, his half-brother, powerful newspaper owner Richard, and Angela's grandson Lance.

General Hospital
ATV
1972–1979
A later update of the *Emergency Ward 10*-style soap, this series was first shown twice-weekly in afternoons, but moved to an hour-long peak slot.

Neighbours
The Reg Grundy Organisation
1985–
Coronation Street Down Under, this explores the activities on Ramsay Street, particularly those of Max Ramsay and his family, after whom the street is named.

Peyton Place
ABC
1964–1969
Based on the novels of Grace Metalious, this series followed the lives and loves of the Peyton Place township in New England. Spawned a film.

Santa Barbara
NBC
1984–
Two wealthy families fight to gain control of coastal California city Santa Barbara.

Sons and Daughters
The Reg Grundy Organisation
1982–1986
The Hamiltons and the Palmers, their relations and acquaintances, square off against one another and the nasty Patricia.

The Sullivans
Crawford Productions
1977–1984
An Australian family works and grows through World War II and after.

Take the High Road
STV
1980–
Most of the action takes place in the village shop in this series, based on a small fictional Scottish village, Glendaroch.

Triangle
BBC
1981–1982
This failed series based its episodes around a passenger fleet of ships running between three North Sea ports.

The Waltons
CBS
1972–1981
An all-American family fights to make a living in the depression years of the 1930s. Set in the Blue Ridge Mountains of Virginia.

The Young Doctors
The Reg Grundy Organisation
1976–
This Australian drama, set in the Albert Memorial Hospital, follows the goings-on amongst a group of (not all young) doctors, their families, friends and patients.

Bibliography

Periodicals

Celebrity, D.C. Thompson, London.
The National Enquirer, The National
 Enquirer Inc., Lantana, Florida.
Radio Times, BBC Publications, London.
Telegraph Sunday Magazine, the Daily
 Telegraph.
TV Times, ITV Publications, London.
Weekend, Mail Newspaper Group, London.
The Weekly News, D.C. Thompson,
 London.

Books

H.V. Kewshaw, *The Street Where I Live*.
 London: Granada Publishing, 1986.
Tony Lynch, *EastEnders Special*. London:
 Grand Dreams, 1986.
Keith Miles, *Crossroads Special*. London:
 Grand Dreams, 1982.
Graham Nown, *Coronation Street: The First
 25 Years*. London: Ward Lock, 1985.
Christopher Schemering, *The Soap Opera
 Encyclopedia*. New York: Ballantine,
 1985.
Laura van Wormer, *Dynasty*. London:
 Comet Books, 1983.
Laura van Wormer, *Dallas*. London and
 New York: Comet Books, 1985.
Laura van Wormer, *Knots Landing*. New
 York: Doubleday, 1986.

Soap Fan's Quiz – Answers

EastEnders
Q1. B
Q2. C
Q3. A
Q4. B
Q5. B

Dallas
Q1. C
Q2. A
Q3. C
Q4. B
Q5. C

Coronation Street
Q1. B
Q2. A
Q3. C
Q4. B
Q5. C

Dynasty
Q1. B
Q2. A
Q3. C
Q4. B
Q5. C

Crossroads
Q1. B
Q2. C
Q3. A
Q4. B
Q5. A

The Colbys
Q1. B
Q2. A
Q3. C
Q4. B
Q5. C

Brookside
Q1. C
Q2. B
Q3. A
Q4. B
Q5. A

Knots Landing
Q1. B
Q2. C
Q3. A
Q4. B
Q5. C

Emmerdale Farm
Q1. B
Q2. C
Q3. A
Q4. C
Q5. C

Index

Listed below are the names of the actors and actresses who are the stars of Supersoaps. The characters they play are given in brackets. *Italic* page numbers refer to illustrations.